MW00817582

Sovereignty, War, and the Global State

Dylan Craig

Sovereignty, War, and the Global State

palgrave
macmillan

Dylan Craig
School of International Service
American University
Washington, DC, USA

ISBN 978-3-030-19885-5   ISBN 978-3-030-19886-2   (eBook)
https://doi.org/10.1007/978-3-030-19886-2

This Palgrave Macmillan imprint is published by the registered company Springer Nature Switzerland AG
The registered company address is: Gewerbestrasse 11, 6330 Cham, Switzerland

ACKNOWLEDGMENTS

This book is the product of nine years of consistent focus on the conduct of violence by states using irregular forces in geopolitically complex conditions. During that time, I have benefited greatly from the mentorship and support of teachers and peers too numerous to mention individually. In particular, however, I want to thank Isabelle Duyvesteyn, who provided me with my first collegial contact outside my home institution and showed me how intellectual exchange was meant to work; Ken Menkhaus, who first impressed on me the importance of moving quickly on my intuitions about proxy war after we spoke at a conference in 2009; Philip Brenner and Chuck Call, who bought me many lunches and coffees when days were dark and graduate student funds were few; Boaz Atzili, for providing a calm and inspiring voice in our many discussions of proxy war; and Maria Green Cowles, who hired me on at the School of International Service in 2011 and made my further scholarly work on this topic financially possible.

In more ways than one, this book owes its existence to Janice E. Thomson's *Mercenaries, Pirates and Sovereigns* and Theda Skocpol's *States and Social Revolutions*, both of which inspired me and showed me how patterns in history could be leveraged to provide interesting insights into the world of international relations.

Portions of the research that went into this book were conducted under a Dean's Summer Research Grant from American University in 2015, and a residential fellowship from the Irmgard Coninx Stiftung in 2012. I am deeply indebted to both institutions for their support.

On the home front, this book could not have been written without the love and support of my family: my spouse Karen, our dog Thandi, and our children Freya and Alexa, who were born around the time I first proposed this topic to Palgrave Macmillan, and who have turned into fierce and wonderful little toddlers before my eyes as the manuscript progressed. I hope that the world of your futures is at least a more understandable place, and perhaps even a safer and kinder place, than the world described in these pages.

Lastly, I dedicate this book to my parents, Anita and Denham, without whom none of this would have been possible.

Introduction

On the morning of November 10, 1589, in a field near Smerwick Castle, 600 Spanish and Italian soldiers and their camp followers were formed into groups and methodically executed by English troops. Had these soldiers been taken prisoner on some Continental battlefield, they might well have called for mercy and had it granted, but this battle was different. The captured troops were not there under the auspices of their faraway states; instead, they were part of a Papal expeditionary force sent to support the Irish Catholic forces of the Second Desmond Rebellion. From the point of view of their executioners, then, these were not enemy combatants in the usual sense, but rebels against the legitimate authority of the Queen, and thus outside the usual norms relating to the treatment of captives.

In May 2015, a Ukrainian member of parliament used Facebook and YouTube to offer the repatriation of Alexander Alexandrov and Yevgeny Yerofeyev, two Russian soldiers captured by Ukrainian forces during the Crimean separatist conflict, in exchange for around 400 Ukrainians being held by Russian and separatist forces.[1] Such an exchange would not have been without precedent: the year before, 63 Ukrainian prisoners of war had been exchanged for a unit of 10 Russian paratroopers taken captive after a firefight with Ukrainian Special Forces. The two men were indeed freed and repatriated, but only after a year of negotiations, with Russian authorities maintaining the whole time that the two men were in Ukraine as volunteers and not as part of the Russian military, and Ukrainian authorities responding by charging Alexandrov and Yerofeyev with terrorism and sentencing them to a 14-year prison term.

Several striking parallels connect these two events, not least of which are the hazards faced by individuals who find themselves caught with one foot in the world of international relations and the other in the world of civil war. If the Russian example seems to imply that these hazards have diminished in intensity since the siege of Smerwick, the fatal experiences of Chadian "mercenaries" captured by rebel forces in the Libyan civil war, or the fates of "foreign fighters" and "illegal combatants" interned indefinitely in Guantanamo Bay by the US military, should make it clear that this is not necessarily the case.

What has happened in the last 400 years, though, is that several epochal transitions have been initiated in attempts to regulate or mitigate the character of the kinds of grand conflict judged to be of the highest concern to states and other significant actors in the global system. These transitions, instantiated by conventions such as the Peace of Westphalia (1648) or the Atlantic Charter (1941), have so frequently and dramatically drawn and redrawn the lines around who may fight, where, and how, that it can seem to us that the sixteenth and the twenty-first century are so different as to be incomparable, and that contemporary conflicts are leading us into a future of sui generis insecurity.

In this book, I show that the reverse is true. Smerwick and Crimea are not only linked by a string of shadowy struggles conducted in the interstices and gray zones of formalized war, or more aptly in the "negative spaces" of each of the great war-regulating sovereign orders, but their respective worlds of war are also linked by recurring characteristics among the fighters who are recruited to serve in these interstices. States have changed greatly in the last 400 years: interstitial fighters have changed far less, and the same can be said of the recurring styles in which their powerful patrons employ them to go where those patrons cannot. By charting these continuities—and three important discontinuities, namely the filibuster, the armed drone, and "proxy war by proxy"—I show how recognizing interstitial war for what it is not only clarifies much concerning our contemporary world at war, but also provides a clear path forward in legal, military, and scholarly terms.

Structure of the Book

This book is divided into six chapters, split over three sections as follows.

- The first section, which contains Chap. 1, presents a review of literature applicable to the phenomenon of interstitial war as well as my
  own model of the <u>sovereign interstice</u>.
- The second section contains Chaps. 2, 3, and 4, in which I subject a
  range of cases of interstitial warfare to analysis by means of a historical narrative approach. My task in each of these chapters is to investigate a different phase or incarnation of interstitial warfare,
  distinguishable from one another by the different relationship they
  show between the violent actors and the interstice in which they are
  fighting. Have the actors created the interstice anew, in order to pursue forms of violence that would otherwise be illegal or impractical
  outside it (Chap. 2)? Are they attempting to exploit an existing interstice in pursuit of specific benefits (Chap. 3)? Are they attempting to
  close a troublesome interstice and return the area to the formal jurisdiction of a single state (Chap. 4)? Each chapter juxtaposes several
  cases in order to draw out the key characteristics that connect the
  actions of the interstitial actors in question, and thereby lay bare the
  processes by which interstices open, persist, or close.
- The third section contains Chaps. 5 and 6, in which I consider apparent "tough cases" for my model, that is, the filibusters, drones, and
  "proxy war by proxy" mentioned earlier. I use these tough cases to
  identify the prospects for considering how a persistent system of
  interstitial war might have changed over time; I then take this inves-
  tigation further to develop the notion of a "dynamic sovereign
  order" in Chap. 6.

Note

1. Alec Luhn. November 2017. "Russian soldiers" captured in Ukraine to face
   trial on terrorism charges, *The Guardian*. https://www.theguardian.com/
   world/2015/may/18/russian-soldiers-ukraine-trial-terrorism-charges.
   Accessed February 2, 2019.

CONTENTS

ABOUT THE AUTHOR

Dylan Craig is Senior Professorial Lecturer of International Relations in the School of International Service. His recent research projects have concerned proxy wars, the intermediarization of violence more generally, and the "sovereign interstices" to which these intermediarized forms of violence are adapted. Before joining the School of International Service community in 2004, he taught colonial and Cold War history at Rhodes University in South Africa.

LIST OF FIGURES

LIST OF TABLES

The Intellectual Context

Although the notion of interstitial war that I advance in this book is a novel one, several large and well-explored areas of study provide useful conceptual tools for understanding what I mean by a sovereign interstice, and where existing models come closest to explaining the same kinds of violence that I am concerned with here.

In this chapter, I bring these useful conceptual tools and applicable models together under three headings. I begin by considering various key perspectives on "war, the state, and the state of war"[1] within fields such as political science, military history, and international relations. Following this, I use insights from the fields of political geography (specifically, John Agnew's notion of sovereignty regimes) to add a systemic and spatial dimension to these key perspectives on warfare, such that the utility of thinking about the locatedness of outwardly directed state violence both in physical place and social space becomes clear. Finally, I introduce and specify the key elements of my own model of the sovereign interstice, whose application to the cases collected in Chaps. 2, 3, and 4 forms the core of this book.

War

In his 1964 introduction to the new edition of Quincy Wright's *A Study of War*, Karl Deutsch wrote that "[nothing] less than ... the understanding of war and the possible ways to its abolition ... is on the agenda of our

© The Author(s) 2020
D. Craig, *Sovereignty, War, and the Global State,*
https://doi.org/10.1007/978-3-030-19886-2_1

time."[2] Five decades later, we are still trying to "understand" war; however, the important thing about Deutsch's statement is not just its ambition (i.e., that war would be understood for once and for all during "our time"), but rather the very notion that war could be treated as a phenomenon in its own right rather than only a by-product of bigger structures such as politics, human nature, class exploitation, or "racial" destiny.

Before works such as *A Study of War*, the notion that two regionally and historically distinct episodes of conflict might be assigned functional equivalence through their reduction into a set of salient characteristics (e.g., type of regimes at war, number of fatalities), and directly studied to determine common inputs or outputs, was unknown. Less than 50 years later, however, this practice is so common as to be second nature to the war enumerator. In this regard, Wright and those who have continued to build on his work (such as Small and Singer) have indeed changed the way that we study war.

However, once we take Wright, Richardson, Small, and Singer at their word, and accept the notion that "war" is a regular enough phenomenon that scholars should direct effort toward enumerating wars, assembling them into datasets, and comparing them, we soon find that the very task of defining what counts as an incidence of "war" is itself a process bedeviled by different and competing perspectives on, theories of, methods for the study of, and thus definitions of war. While Wright and Richardson confronted this challenge through their own methods, they did not do so in ways that have settled the question, "what is war?"

Different perspectives on this question thus persist: and in choosing between (or combining) these competing perspectives, we find ourselves having to ask a range of questions. Is war to be primarily understood in terms of the actors/agents involved (who fights, why they fight, how they fight), or is it caused by various systemic features? Has war changed in nature over time and depending on context, or is its nature timeless? Last, and specifically important given the particular focus of the present project: how can we decide whether a given sequence or cluster of widespread, violent events (e.g., the decolonization conflicts in Africa) is best understood as (i) war, (ii) some particular or a unique kind of war, distinct from other particular/unique kinds, or (iii) some other kind of phenomenon entirely?

Arguing in in favor of a broader and more inclusive definition of war, Joseph Salerno argues that war obtains whenever some have power and others do not:

We thus arrive at a universal, praxeological truth about war: it is the out-come of ... conflict inherent in the political relationship—the relationship between ruler and ruled ... [the] parasitic class—the rulers; their police, military, and civil servants; and their supporting special-interest coalition(s)—makes war with purpose and deliberation in order to conceal and ratchet up its exploitation ... the conflict between ruler and ruled is a permanent condition.[3]

A similarly cross-cutting perspective is employed by Robert Layton when he argues, from an anthropological perspective, that

[h]uman warfare arises when the web of social relationship is compromised. Human societies are complex systems and vulnerable to periods of disorder ... [the] manipulative activities of leaders play a part in fomenting war, whether they are local Big Men in small-scale, decentralized societies or the leaders of nation states.[4]

Lastly, Charles Tilly takes a different route than Salerno and Layton, but arrives at the same destination, that is, that we should loosen the stric-tures around what we count as "war," and what kinds of groups can be thought of as waging it. In *The Politics of Collective Violence*,[5] for example, Tilly identifies six different types of collective, interpersonal violence: bro-ken negotiations, opportunism, brawls, scattered attacks, violent rituals, and coordinated destruction.[6] When the latter three kinds of violence co-occur, Tilly calls this composite phenomenon "war," and in so doing pro-duces a conception of war that applies to the contemporary, High Modern, and classical battlefield alike.

Various approaches to capturing the diversity of "war" thus exist, but none conclusively settles the debate around what to think of as war. As Vasquez points out, some of our difficulties in defining war stem simply from the fact that "war" is a <u>noun</u> in the English language rather than a verb.[7] After all, war conceived of as an institution, or phenomenon, in its own right (i.e., "war" used as a noun), permits different routes of inquiry than war conceived of as a relational,[8] inter-institutional behavior—that is, "war" used as a verb or "warfare" to focus on the use of war rather than war itself.

However, this distinction (and the associated definitional back-and-forth over "war") notwithstanding, we still find ourselves in need of some kind of working definition of war in order to identify it for further study. Wright and Richardson inaugurated the use of threshold numbers of deaths in battle as the sign that a war was taking place, and many (starting with Small and Singer) have followed their route. However, I want to specifically draw attention to Istvan Kende's operationalization of war as useful for the work I conduct in this book. Kende writes:

We define war as any armed conflict in which all of the following criteria obtain:

> Activities of regular armed forces (military, police forces, etc.) at least on one side—that is, the presence and engagement of the armed forces of the government in power;
> A certain degree of organization and organized fighting on both opposing sides, even if this organization extends to organized defence [sic] only;
> A certain continuity between the armed clashes, however sporadic. Centrally organized guerilla forces are also regarded as making war, insofar as their activities extend over a considerable part of the country concerned.[9]

This definition of war is particularly interesting to me because Kende was specifically attempting to fit a concept dominated by its statist origins (i.e., war) around a body of empirical data in which states were playing an increasingly non-exclusive role. Indeed, writing in 1978, Kende saw in his data the emergence of a very <u>particular</u> kind of war:

> The current main type of wars is the anti-regime (A) type war, mainly with foreign participation (Category A/I) ... [we] have stressed the importance of the change which made this kind into the main type of war instead of the border wars which dominated in the past. The fact that type A but mainly type A/I wars are in such a majority is an unequivocal consequence of the current political situation.[10]

Kende's "Category A/I" wars thus embody many of the features of interstitial war to be discussed in what follows, and the same goes for his definition, which attempted to leave space both for states and non-states in the practice of war. For this reason, and without implying that war must include the state by definition, we can nonetheless observe in the diverse works of Tilly, Salerno, Vasquez, and Layton mentioned earlier that war and the actions of large political collectives go hand in hand. We thereby find ourselves agreeing with Kende's implication (via the first element of his definition) that whatever else we think we "understand" about war, we can be confident that it in some way continues to feature the pursuit of objectives by states. I turn to what it means to talk of states as entities pursuing objectives next.

THE STATE

Max Weber's *Politics As a Vocation* outlines four characteristics of a state: (i) it is constituted by its means rather than its goals; (ii) these means are founded in violence; (iii) the violence must be acceded to or legitimated by the governed; and (iv) a clear differentiation is to be found between different states based on the overlap between ownership of the material and immaterial technologies of violence.[11] Furthermore, for Weber, the institutional and territorial boundaries of the associated society are the same. Indeed, "[t]erritory is a characteristic of the state."[12]

With reference to the specific issue of how to define the state, it must be noted that subsequent work on the state has focused on different characteristics than Weber's. Where Weber identifies the establishment of a stable coercive monopoly as a key element in the creation of what we today recognize as "states," Roberto Unger's *Plasticity into Power*, for example, suggests the opposite: polities in which the rulers found it too easy to defend themselves against the people are precisely those which tended to stagnate and fragment over history, to be replaced by more durable egalitarian polities.[13]

While Unger and Weber are arguing from different positions on the role of coercion, they share the idea that we might best understand the state by observing its successes or failures at establishing a coercive monopoly. In contrast, and as a third perspective on how to recognize and delineate the state for further study, Joel Migdal's work on the state advances a "state-in-society" model, in which rather than being an actual or would-be coercive monopolist, the state is just one (albeit usually the most powerful) actor in a "*mélange*" of competing institutions.

Rather than attempting to discredit the coercion-related analyses of Unger and others,[14] Migdal cautions against becoming confused between models or ideal types of the state, and attempts to characterize <u>actual</u> states: "[in] short, Weber's ideal state when taken as the normal state obscures as much as it illuminates by continually measuring actual states against the ideal version of what states are or ought to be."[15] This is accomplished by tracking and accounting for those legitimacy-based struggles within a society that define a "state-society boundary."[16] Migdal's *mélange*, although he does not put it in exactly these terms, also reverses Weber's assertion about territory being a characteristic of the state, and instead asks: "how are we to describe those situations where, as a consequence of various limitations on the exercise of state power, the formal state is just one characteristic of a territorially bounded society?"

Following the insights of Weber, Migdal, Unger, and other scholars, three opposing camps can thus be said to exist as far as defining the state goes: (i) that the state is a cluster of territorialized institutions backed up by their monopolized command over the legitimacy of coercion; (ii) that the state is an exerciser of social power, fulfilling key functions and providing collective goods to its subjects; and (iii) that the state is just one element in a web of state-society relations, serving as a broker and representative to a range of groups within its jurisdictions.[17]

Although these three approaches highlight different aspects of the state, in the case of many states they are not mutually exclusive. States can, for example, employ coercive monopolies as well as provide public goods and coordinate the activities of sub-state interest groups. On the other hand, these conceptions do not accord well (either individually or together) with the specific realities of "limited," "weak," or "failed" states. Indeed, these definitions fall conspicuously short when applied, for example, to much of the developing (or, postcolonial) world. In these areas, states have neither coercive monopolies, nor much social power, nor even a privileged relationship of brokerage with their citizens as such. Instead, the "politics of dysfunction" sustain the operation of "kleptocracies" or "chaosocracies,"[18] in which the organs of state (including the means to war) are little more than neopatrimonial currency, parceled out to promising clients.

These signs of states failing to match the monolithic Weberian ideal type are not the sole province of limited, weak, or failing states. Indeed, Susan Strange characterizes the modern state in general as one often unable to "discharge those very basic functions for which the state institution was created—the maintenance of civil law and order, [and] the defence of the territory from the depredations of invaders."[19] However, scholars of weak states have taken advantage of widespread state dysfunction in locations such as postcolonial African states to drive the best of current knowledge on the low-capacity state even further.

Jeffrey Herbst, for example, uses geopolitical analyses and population density data to link the pre-colonial, colonial, and postcolonial political dispensations of African states, to the challenges of broadcasting power over a distance.[20] Not only do many states in Africa grapple with political geographies which make this task harder than it might otherwise be—remote and hard-to-govern hinterlands, a lack of transport infrastructure, and so on—but the difficulties of taxing hinterland populations, as well as the imperatives associated with Migdal's "politics of survival," mean that there are precious few incentives to reverse this situation. Between the internationally guaranteed (*de jure*) borders of the state and the practical (*de facto*) extent of metropolitan interest/power, thus spring up the modern equivalents of those areas that French colonizers once called *Africa inutile*: "useless Africa." These areas are stuck in a vicious circle: they are not worth governing because they have no infrastructure, and they have no infrastructure because they are not worth governing.

We can thus add another dimension to our assessment of the accommodations employed by low-capacity states to preserve what agency they can, and that is accommodations made necessary (or attractive) by the complex, non-monolithic spatialization of the state. Put differently: not only do the socio-infrastructural factors discussed by Weber, Migdal, Herbst, and Unger matter in explaining why some states depart from the Weberian ideal, but physical and human geographies also play a role. Sometimes the state is <u>socio-infrastructurally</u> unable to govern all its space; sometimes, it is <u>geographically</u> unable to do so; and sometimes, these inabilities interact in novel ways.[21]

Modern states, however, exist neither entirely on an abstract plane of institutions, nor only in terms of their own more-or-less governance-restricting internal geography; rather, they exist in a world containing many other states, groups, and entities. To understand the state, then, we cannot simply consider its internal actions and accommodations; we must also consider its actions external to itself. Of the various analyses that are concerned with how interactions between these other states, groups, and entities may affect the degrees of accommodation present in the low-capacity state, I single out William Reno's *Warlord Politics and African States* for review here.[22]

Reno is concerned with explaining how "tax evasion, barter deals, illicit production, smuggling, and protection rackets ... have become widespread and integral to building political authority in parts of Africa."[23] Primarily, he says that this is because of an interaction between particular state inability (e.g., an inability to extract wealth from one's hinterland), on the one hand, and the constant presence of external actors—intergovernmental organizations, criminal networks, and foreign multinationals—who <u>are</u>

capable of this. Reno's recognition of this global dimension brings to our understanding of accommodations an awareness of the fact that African states have more options on hand than simply to "govern" versus "not govern." That is to say, they can also make accommodations, that is, partnerships outside the state (either territorially, institutionally, or both), thereby "renting" (although perhaps "pawning" is a better term) their troublesome, valuable, or hard-to-exploit national assets to intermediaries who are willing to pay for the privilege of extracting value from them.

The reason that Reno considers these partnerships to be problematic is that they reinforce the very kinds of state weakness which made them possible (or attractive) in the first place. Because these intermediaries provide an easy alternative to the difficult "politics of survival," rulers are tempted to engage with them (thereby building a "shadow state") rather than working to construct the kinds of domestic partnerships that would serve to strengthen state-society relations. Thus,

> [t]he feature that most distinguishes the building of political authority in weak states and warlord political units in Africa from the early modern European experience is the absence of an indigenous social alliance with which rulers must bargain in exchange for resources. The use of external actors as stand-ins for mobilizing local populations makes violence in warlord strategies rather different from that in early modern European state building.[24]

If Herbst's analysis established the salience of human and physical geography in explaining the various weaknesses and incapabilities to which states might respond through the creation of partnerships intended to compensate for the impossibility of following the Weberian model under the circumstances in which these states find themselves, then Reno's work on the shadow state highlights the fact that in a globalized world, it is not only domestic, civil-society groups who can be partnered with in such accommodations, but also foreign states, actors outside the state (such as warlords), and the representatives of international or transnational groups.

Combining Weber, Unger, Migdal, Herbst, and Reno, we therefore have a sense that while some states may in principle elect to exhibit a kind of coercive autarky, using only their own powers to safeguard key internal and external resources and destroying any rivals to this autarky, all states in practice have at least the option of making accommodations with partners at home or abroad; and furthermore, that the more pressing the threats a state faces, and/or the less it is able to rely on its own powers to get what it wants, the more likely it is to take advantage of this option. Combining this insight with our three-part definition of war from Kende, we can imagine the wars of such "accommodation-seeking states" as featuring (i) a mix of formal and informal forces, (ii) loosely coordinated in service of the state's goals, and (iii) engaging in a series of violent acts from whose continuity these goals can be inferred. As it happens, this precisely describes the bulk of warfare throughout recorded history; I outline this "state of war" next.

THE STATE OF WAR

The analysis that I have conducted earlier is by no means the first to concede that actual warfare involves more than just a clash between ideal-typical Weberian states. Indeed, even in the extremely ideal-type-adherent works of Carl von Clausewitz (to whom we will return in Chap. 6), one finds the acknowledgment that

> [t]he half-civilized Tartars, the republics of antiquity, the feudal lords and commercial cities of the Middle Ages, kings of the eighteenth century, and, finally, princes and peoples of the nineteenth century all waged war in their own way, conducted it differently, with different means, and for different aims.[25]

Neither is it the case that this book is the first to point out that wars can feature heterogeneous (i.e., a mix of state and non-state) alliances, albeit that conflict scholarship does seem to periodically rediscover this in waves of crashing epiphany rather than maintaining it as a standing truth from decade to decade. Mary Kaldor's "horizontal coalitions of breakaway [regular] units, local militia or self-defence units, criminal gangs, groups of fanatics, and hangers-on"[26] and Martin Van Creveld's notion of non-trinitarian fighting forces[27] are prominent elements of the most recent renewal of scholarship on this facet of modern war, as is (more recently) David Kilcullen's concept of "nested hybridity."[28] For all these authors, it is likewise an unproblematic assertion that states and non-states have different repertoires of military action, from the fire-mobility-shock tactics of formal fighting forces to the broad and diffuse violence of the insurgent; and if non-states sometimes attempt to conduct state-like wars of conquest and capture,[29] or states sometimes attempt to learn to fight like guerrillas,[30] all the more interesting.

If this latest crop of theories about wars conducted through partnerships can be said to be missing anything, it is thus not that they miss interesting elements of contemporary conflict; but rather that, as we will see quite well in Chap. 3, drawing on international insurgent networks to field hybrid armies that are part-bandit, part-soldier is nothing that Louis XIV's seventeenth-century generals would have failed to recognize, or that a fourteenth-century Ottoman Sultan would be unable to relate to. In other words, modern theories about conflicts that deviate from the ideal-typical mold tend not to engage with their topic further back than the twentieth century. This forces the theorists (and their readers) into one of two unproductive dead ends, either unable to extract an otherwise useful model from its entangling historical context, as is the case with studies of "proxy war" outside of its superpower-sponsored Cold War incarnation[31]; or, unable to see that many forms of modern violence only look new, unprecedented, and unpredictable when nineteenth-century Europe is treated as neutral baseline instead of a highly contingent outcome.

There is in fact, as this book shows, very little about twenty-first-century war across the globe that is unprecedented once one moves further back in history than the Battle of Waterloo. Thus, what should really give is pause about any theory that irrevocably locates the origins of complex conflicts in definitively modern phenomena, is the concern that a reductive presentism has led its authors to missing something older and more fundamental about how and when states turn to non-states for the purposes of war.

The power of the twentieth-century European experience to deform our notions of the generic and universal is a problem in more fields than war studies. Speaking about studies of state formation, for example, Roberto Unger put it like this:

> Whatever departs from [the Western] stereotype is made to appear a deviation, qualifying or delaying an inexorable developmental tendency. But the argument of this essay turns this prejudice upside down ... [the] supposed anomalies were and are the real Western thing.[32]

As I will argue later in the chapter, when it comes to conflict studies there is one element of the twentieth-century European experience that contributes disproportionately to the field's problems with presentism, and that is what we might call its spatial ontology—that is, its sense of where interstate phenomena like war take place. I explore the legacy of the late nineteenth and early twentieth century's problematic ontological baggage next.

LOCATEDNESS

When our scholarly investigations of conflict engage with location at all, they do so within a basically two-dimensional image—a chessboard with states as the non-overlapping squares. Thus, conflict actors can be "close to" or "far from" one another, and this can have effects on, for example, who perceives threats from whom, or allies with whom.[33] We also have a sense, from our chess board, of a the world as a battlefield with flanks and sides; thus, a state might be recognized as a buffer state because it is "between" two others, and we might then ask questions, for example, about its likely foreign policy choices, or the relative survival chances of such states over time.[34] Even more importantly: because of this image, individual conflict events or prolonged campaigns are thought of as playing out either "within" or "at" the contact surfaces (i.e., borders) between recognized entities. This distinction is then baked into the quantitative databases upon which most broad-scope work is done[35]: conflicts might thus be classified as "interstate," "intrastate," "extrasystemic," or "intrastate with external involvement" based on where they take place relative to the borders between recognized geopolitical entities—that is, between squares, within one square, on the edge of the board, a mix of between and within. But these classifications do more than serve as a raw typology for classifying events; they also become containers for clusters of scholarship, enabling phrases like "a review of theories of interstate war," "a fuller grasp of the civil war literature," and so on.

All of this is fine and well for scholarship focusing on eras in which the bipolar model is a sensible one, and in which the relationship between the physical (i.e., empirical) and social (i.e., juridical) boundaries of the dominant war-making entities has been relatively clear and unambiguous—for example, Western Europe between 1870 and 1941. In this kind of environment, it is indeed possible to draw a relatively sharp contrast between internal or revolutionary conflicts, on the one hand, and those between states on the other. Indeed, within such eras one could go so far as to say that the links between space, place, and war are not only pervasive but also reciprocally reinforcing: states fight <u>to</u> expand their empirical and juridical boundaries, and they do so by fighting <u>on</u> those boundaries and reallocating them, one square mile or kilometer at a time, from the formal control of one state to the formal control of another. To repurpose Tilly's aphorism: territorial wars make the territorial state, and the territorial state makes territorial wars.

On either side of periods like the late nineteenth and early twentieth century, though, we rapidly run into problems directly equating space, place, and war. On the one hand, great powers extend military force and the commensurate right to self-defense regionally or even globally—one might well ask where the twenty-first-century US borders "are," practically, or where Great Britain's were in the eighteenth century, or one might fail to see the humor when Russian President Vladimir Putin jokes that Russia's borders "do not end anywhere"[36]—and on the other hand, states with a more or less notional control of their own jurisdictions either struggle against, ignore, or even actively nurture violence-capable transnational actors operating from their own uncontrolled hinterlands and "ungoverned spaces." We call these struggling states "failed," but what we often mean is "geopolitically incoherent in ways that produce security problems." For these states, and for the neighbors and global community surrounding them, the effects of the mismatch between borders and wars is a clear analytical and practical challenge to any models of conflict that revolve solely around concepts such as "interstate" or "intrastate."

My most specific objection is to the idea that wars occurring "inside" the state must be civil wars, or at least that they must be so different from wars occurring "outside" the state that they should be studied in isolation from such wars. This assumption strips the historical record of a great many interstate wars simply because these happen within the context of (or, one might say, concealed by) a "civil" or intrastate war. With the historical record thus denuded, we lose the ability, as conflict scholars, to accurately investigate war-making by and between states; hence we lose the ability to grapple, for example, with Kilcullen's "nested, irregular" conflicts, or with the conflicts attendant to Reno's shadow state.

As if this were not problematic enough, calibrating our study of war on the inter-intrastate notion facilitates two further practices which only further muddy the waters around complex hybrid conflicts.

First, conflict study projects that were inaugurated during the Cold War and that have persisted afterwards rely heavily on country-year dyads to indicate that either a state of war exists between country A and country B in year C (an interstate conflict), or that a state of war exists between government A and rebel faction B in year C (in intrastate conflict). This is a defensible decision in many cases, but it is a methodological rather than a theoretical one; that is to say, it is driven primarily by a need to render the world susceptible to statistical, large-n analysis (i.e., to operationalize it) rather than out of an attempt to specify its nature and causal mechanisms (i.e., to <u>define</u> it). Hence, when the very nature of conflict changes, there is no intrinsic reason to assume that previous operationalizations of conflict will continue to "point" our research instruments, as it were, toward the right phenomena or conclusions regarding conflict.

<u>Second</u>, while projects such as the UCDP-PRIO (Uppsala Conflict Data Program and the Peace Research Institute Oslo)[37] conflict dataset have increasingly begun to include a category for "civil wars with foreign intervention," the pernicious effects of the conceptual division between "interstate" and "intrastate" wars act to weaken the conclusions that can be derived even from this step in the right direction. For example, in reading a recent annual report from the Stockholm International Peace Reseach Institute (SIPRI), one sees that the rise in interventionary conflicts (i.e., states' meddling in one another's "civil" wars) is one of the project's key findings.[38] This conclusion is corroborated by Kilcullen's more qualitative findings, and there is no indication that we should treat it with undue skepticism. When the time comes to draw this conclusion together with other trends, however, the trend abruptly disappears—not because it is defeated by data, but because the report uses only three categories for its summary of trends in violent conflict: "state-based conflict," "non-state conflict," and "one-sided violence" between governments and populations. Seen through this lens, interventionary conflicts disappear into the category of "non-state conflict" and the data for this category is used to sustain the conclusions that (a) the incidence of interstate wars has dropped off since the end of the Cold War, and (b) the incidence of intrastate wars, after a spike in the 1990s, has leveled out. However, this conclusion makes little sense if states are actually fighting one another by inflaming and stirring up one another's internal conflicts; indeed, if this is the case, we would be just as correct if we interpreted the SIPRI data as suggesting that interstate war had *increased* in frequency and that intrastate war—actual, non-interventionary internal war—had *decreased*. Until we correct our assumptions about how the social and physical location of war maps onto its nature—in other words, until we correct our <u>spatial ontology of war</u>—we will be unable to conclusively find in favor of either of these conclusions over the other.

Two interesting trends bear mentioning as far as the search for a new, and more adequate spatial ontology of conflict goes: first, the advent of more sophisticated geographic information systems (GIS) tools has allowed some conflict scholars to step away from the state as the sole locator of conflict, replacing it, for example, with a neutral grid onto which geolocated conflict events are imposed, thereby allowing for examinations of how different types of conflict interact with geography or population density[39]; and, second, the work produced by conflict scholars who have attempted to re-theorize interventionary "intrastate" conflict in some way, such as by developing new models of hybrid, nested rivalries in which triads of actors rather than the more problematic dyads, form the key analytic unit.[40] Both of these approaches seem likely to produce a more effective way forward. In my own work on the topic, and as a core element of the approach taken in this book, I wish to add a third approach, which is to think about conflict not in terms of a chessboard as mentioned previously, but in three dimensions, that is, as a series of overlaps, overhangs, and shadows formed by states projecting the area they claim authority to up and over other states that are doing the same. This is an adaptation of political geographer John Agnew's model of the "sovereignty regime"; I explore this model and its capacity to refresh the spatial ontology of conflict studies next.

SOVEREIGNTY REGIMES

As we saw in the discussion of the state earlier, the scholarly idea that "[t]erritory is a characteristic of the state" goes back to Weber[41]; in this vision of the state, the institutional and the territorial boundaries of the associated society are therefore the same. In describing the fall of the Weberian state along these lines, scholars such as Herbst and Jackson have described a pulling away or reconfiguration of the de facto state (i.e., the state as actor able to effect its will) from its de jure boundaries (i.e., the boundaries within which it is entitled to act in this way) to form an archipelago of "quasi-states" adrift in a sea of ungovernable "hinterlands."[42]

An alternative approach taken by John Agnew probes the core assumption that such a thing as "de jure" sovereignty even exists in any measurable sense.[43] Agnew writes:

> The questioning of territorial de jure sovereignty matters not simply because of the challenge to state political primacy from globalization but because the equation of state with sovereignty is intrinsic to the ways in which politics in general and democracy in particular have been considered in modern times.[44]

War as a social practice, as an activity participated in by political collectives, is certainly an example of the kind of collective action which an adjustment of our view of territorial sovereignty would allow us to better understand. In what follows, then, I review Agnew's alternative conception of sovereignty as a range of regimes, in order to apply it to the study of heterogeneous military partnerships and the wars they feature in.

Agnew begins by defining political authority as "the legitimate practice of power."[45] A state which is "strong," in terms of his measurement of state authority, is one which successfully deploys legitimate power within its own territory, free of "external dependence and manipulation ... corruption and chronic mismanagement."[46] This political authority can be centralized or diffuse, depending on the precise power structures used to sustain it; as Agnew puts it: "Sovereignty as the legitimate exercise of power (as authority), therefore, is necessarily about ceded, seduced, and co-opted diffused power as well as coercion by (and acceptance of) centralized power."[47]

However, Agnew notes that not all states territorialize (i.e., constitute their space socially and mobilize it politically[48]) in the same way. Agnew makes the following crucial distinction: "All forms of polity ... occupy some sort of space," but qualifies this by saying that "political authority is not necessarily predicated on and defined by strict and fixed territorial boundaries." This goes to the heart of his differentiation between territory and space. The territory of a state is the area which it has territorialized, that is, "used for political, social and economic ends." Territory, therefore, always bears the imprint of the state's power structures, whether these are despotic (charismatic), institutional (bureaucratic), or a blend of the two. Consequently, "territory" may be smaller, larger, or the same as the physical space which the state occupies; it can also exist either as a demarcatable geographic block (when the power structures are centralized), or as a network linked by space-spanning flows of influence (when the power structures are diffuse), or both.

Quoting Spruyt, Agnew argues that not only is it not necessary that the state's space and territory coincide, it is in fact rare: what made the nineteenth- and twentieth-century nation-state so unlike other forms of polity throughout human history, is that it briefly succeeded in making its territory and space synonymous. Primarily, this has to do with the institutions of the state, and whether or not these are "consolidated" (i.e., focused primarily inwards into the state's own territory) or "open" (i.e., focused primarily outwards into the realm of international relations and global trade)—in other words, whether these institutions have been territorialized primarily within the state's geographic and legal boundaries (consolidated), or outside them (open).

John Agnew's notion of a "sovereignty regime" is based on his assessment that a direct correspondence between the political (i.e., authoritative) and spatial (i.e., physical) dimensions of the "state" upon which most of our ideas of "sovereignty" are based, is both a recent and historically bounded phenomenon. Instead of such contiguities, Agnew argues, for the majority of humanity's existence in groups larger than the "band," these dimensions have specifically *not* been the same, whether the political unit in question was a cattle-patronage monarchy in Iron Age Africa, a multiple-jurisdiction guild city in Renaissance Europe, a "failed state," or a modern "hyperpower." Indeed, for every "failed" state whose core institutions occupy *less* space than its territorial boundaries (e.g., Iraq), Agnew points out that there are many states (e.g., the United States) whose institutions are so fundamentally *globalized* that these states are constantly embroiled in battles, whether military or political, to defend them. No-one would call the United States a "failing" or a "quasi"-state, but the fact remains that its juridical and empirical sovereignties are just as dramatically incongruous as Iraq's—albeit that its empirical reach overshadows its juridical reach and not the other way around.

Agnew has produced a four-part typology of these variations, which he calls a typology of "sovereignty regimes" distinguished from one another on axes of increasing authority to act and degree of territorial integration.[49] The two regimes which feature high consolidation are the classic, that is, Weberian-state regime (e.g., China), and the integrative regime (e.g., the EU). What distinguish these two regimes from one another are their different degrees of internal political authority. China, for Agnew, has high authority within its own territory; the EU, because it is constituted from smaller, independent member states, has low authority. Both, however, have an institutional infrastructure which is strongly territorialized within the states' own borders.

A similar division appears among the regimes which Agnew considers to have low consolidation, that is, whose state institutions follow a distributed mode of territorialization. His examples in this regard are the United States (high authority/open, which Agnew calls globalist), and a generic Third World weak/failed state (low authority, open, imperialist). To deal with these in turn: the United States has high amounts of political authority within much of its territory, but the boundaries of this territory are fuzzy because so many of the US interests, wealth, and security needs lie outside the geographical space it nominally inhabits. This engages the United States in a constant struggle for legitimacy as it projects power through and into social and political spaces containing non-citizens (e.g., Iraq). At its worst extent, globalist states become so embroiled in these struggles that they become imperial, destroying other states because they cannot integrate, pacify, or placate them. The result of this destruction is often the generic weak/failed state, which Agnew discusses under the heading of the "imperial" sovereign regime, although "imperialized" might have been a better term. States operating under this kind of sovereignty regime have both dispersed institutions (as they rely on Intergovernmental organizations like the IMF, World Bank, or UN for their continued existence) and no strong domestic power structures of their own. These states are plagued by "separatist threats, local insurgencies, and poor infrastructural integration … infrastructural power is weak or nonexistent, and despotic power is often effectively in outside hands."[50]

In only one of the four variants that Agnew proposes is the state-as-institutional-cluster contained within its own territory alone. In the other three variants, at least some of the institutions upon which the state depends (i.e., which it wishes to dominate, resist, or profit from) lie <u>outside</u> its borders. Thus, for Agnew, sovereignty is a notion best expressed in terms of state's pursuit of regional or even global accommodations, that is, as mixture of domestic/internal and foreign/external relations between the state, and various sources of power or peril which it must manage (i.e., within which it must fight for recognition, control, power, etc.) to survive.

Agnew's model therefore seems to provide us with exactly the new kind of spatial ontology that is needed to get our examinations of the accommodation-seeking state at war past the unproductive interstate-versus-intrastate dichotomy that I have criticized earlier. Accordingly, my model of the sovereign interstice synthesizes the insights of the review of "war, the state, and the state of war" with Agnew's "sovereignty regimes" in order to specifically focus on the partnerships that states create in order to extend their sovereign reach further than they are permitted to. I detail this model by way of concluding this chapter next.

WARFARE AND THE SOVEREIGN INTERSTICE

What is a sovereign interstice? An <u>interstice</u> is a "space between," an area in which contiguity is interrupted by a gap or an overlap: thus, a <u>sovereign interstice</u> is a space in which <u>sovereignty</u> is discontiguous, or in which a gap exists between the nominally exclusive chessboard squares occupied and constituted by recognized geopolitical entities such as states. The

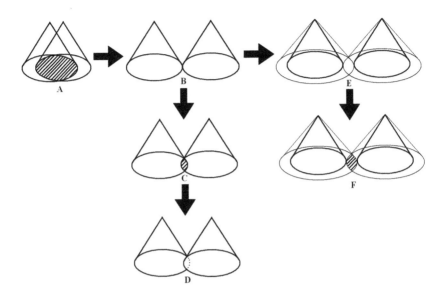

Fig. 1.1 Sovereign conflicts and sovereignties

analysis conducted in this book adds to the notion that if <u>territorial</u> war is the continuation of <u>territorial</u> politics by other means, then <u>interstitial</u> war is the continuation of <u>interstitial</u> politics by other means, that is, the violent incarnation of Agnews' sovereignty regimes. And if we are looking for a way to describe interstate war moving from occurring on the smooth and abstract surfaces between states, to a "ribbon" or "cloud" of mobilizable space between them, then we are discussing a move from war having one kind of "shape" in space and place, to it having another. Figure 1.1 represents this idea.

In this figure, we see the shifting interactions between sovereign states (i.e., territorialized polities) over time, moving from the pre-Westphalian order (<u>configuration A</u>), to the era of the nation-state (<u>configurations B, C, and D</u>), to the increasingly globalized state of the post-World War II "market state"[51] (<u>configurations E and F</u>). Each of these sovereign forms had its own form of endemic conflict. Pre-Westphalian states, in which multiple sovereignties might apply to any particular subject, area, or group, were characterized by constant warring over competing claims to legitimacy. Indeed, "legitimacy" itself was rarely unipolar or exclusive; a medieval warlord might hold titles granted by more than one king, result-

ing in situations in which the warlord would honor his competing obligations by personally serving on one side of a battle while also lending levies
to the other side. Thus, while medieval polities had extensive and intricate
systems of sovereignty, these systems were not configured to be exclusive
of one another, and hence violence—ongoing, brutal, and unpredictable—was a constant reality.[52]

The Peace of Westphalia, in establishing the principle of sovereign invi-
olability, brought an end to the massive religious wars which had dominated early Renaissance Europe. I return to Westphalia in Chap. 6, and
locate it as only one of several large projects of this kind which reconfigured the overlapping medieval rules for the extension of state power in
space; for now, however, suffice it to point out that the precise functioning
of the treaty had less to do with engendering pacifism or religious toler-
ance on the part of its signatories, than it did with the inauguration of a
new phase of en-bordering: one which linked sovereignty to fixed territorial demarcations, thereby separating sovereign entities from another
(configuration B in Fig. 1.1), and enacting a normative and legal ban on
violent intervention in the affairs of one's neighbors.

While violence conducted by sovereigns continued after the Peace, it
differed from the free-ranging violence of the religious zealots, *écorcheurs*,
and marcher lords[53] of the previous era; for in pinning sovereignty to physical space, the Westphalian order welded together the physico-legal foot-
print of the state and its militarized foreign policy, in an arrangement
which would go on to last well into the modern era. The archetype of this
welding-together was the "war of national conquest" (configuration C in
Fig. 1.1), in which the patchwork territorial acquisitions and overlapping
allegiances of the medieval warlords were replaced by the systematic conquest of new lands "for the crown," (configuration D) and later still "for
the empire," and "for the nation," that is, under the flag of the (ever-
evolving) state.

Moving to the globalized state (configuration E), as per work of John
Agnew[54] and Saskia Sassen,[55] globalization has left the modern state
"inside-out": more specifically, while the process of late-Medieval to
Modern statemaking involved states gaining privileged or monopolistic
access to a range of key institutions within their territory, and defending
these from internal and external rivals, the modern state has become fundamentally dependent on extranational circuits and resources for its survival. This is no recent event; one may go so far as to say that even as the
geopolitics of the burgeoning nation-state after Westphalia began to define

each state's de facto and de jure borders, globalization and economic liberalism had already begun to undermine this process, leaving many of the institutions on which states depend (e.g., oil reserves), or to whose defense they are constitutionally committed (e.g., democracy promotion), at various distances beyond their borders.

This brings up a new kind of security problem for the globalized market state: the more broadly the sources of their power are spread around the globe, the more they are forced to exceed their nominal boundaries (either in a de facto or a de jure sense) to defend their core interests; and in almost all cases, this means encroaching on resources or institutions which other states might prefer to keep for themselves (configuration F). For peaceful states, these clashes can be addressed through various forms of multilateralism, such as treaties and intergovernmental organizations[56]; but for states who are tempted to use violence to effect "unilateral, but binding, political decisions,"[57] the path ahead is more complex.

Until 1945, such states could more-or-less legitimately use formal invasion and annexation to secure key extranational resources and defend/construct the institutions that engage with them (configurations C and D in Fig. 1.1); but following the post-World War II ban on "aggressive war," states across the world have found themselves facing a *constraint* on their use of violence without any concomitant decline in the proliferation of reasons for war. This, I contend, has led them to find new strategies for force projection: contractors and militias, state-sponsored terrorism, hybrid and networked warfare (as per Kilcullen)[58] and, especially in regions dominated by low-capacity, affordance-heavy states, proxy war.[59] These seemingly diverse forms of violence have two things in common. First, that they are an attempt, by states, to "go" where the boundaries of the contemporary sovereign order mean they cannot formally "go" (configuration F in Fig. 1.1), and second, with specific reference to our ability to study these conflicts, that their manifestation "within" states masks their interstate origins from the very outset, masking interstate rivalries under the disaffection of local fighters.

To imagine such a thing as "wars of the sovereign interstice," then, is to find oneself searching for a way to articulate violence conducted within gaps between states' empirical reach and their juridical borders. When states fight in these gaps, they do so with a variety of means, but these means are always recognizable by their instrumentality for interstitial action. Furthermore, once we realize that these gaps exist and begin searching within them for regular and repeating patterns, we find that we have at last come full circle back to the injunction by Wright and Deutsch with which I began this chapter: our task is to achieve "the understanding of [interstitial] war," and we will do so by comparing cases which show three recurring ways that states interact with interstices—that is, to open them, to exploit them, or to close them—in the following chapter.

NOTES

1. Here, I am borrowing and adapting the title of Kalevi Holsti's summary of changes in warfare: *The State, War, and the State of War*. Cambridge, UK: Cambridge University Press, 2001.
2. Karl W. Deutsch, 'Quincy Wright's Contribution to the Study of War,' in Quincy Wright, *A Study of War* (USA: University of Chicago Press, 1964), p. xi.
3. Joseph Salerno, 'Imperialism and the Logic of War Making,' *The Independent Review*, 12:3 (Winter 2008), p. 450.
4. Robert Layton, *Order and Anarchy. Civil Society, Social Disorder and War* (USA: Cambridge University Press, 2006), p. 171.
5. Charles Tilly, *The Politics of Collective Violence* (USA: Cambridge University Press, 2003), pp. 34–31.
6. A seventh type (individual aggression) is identified but not explicated, because Tilly's concern is only with those kinds of violence which advance collective goals, and which require *collective* organization.
7. John Vasquez, *The War Puzzle* (Cambridge University Press, 1993), pp. 38–40.
8. That is, founded in a *relationship* between entities (as in "a state of war exists between"), rather than what I call an *attributive* view of war, which makes it an attribute of a region and/or time (e.g., "The Second Schleiswig-Holstein War" or "The Vietnam War").
9. Istvan Kende, "Wars of Ten Years (1967–1976)," *Journal of Peace Research*, Vol. 15, No. 3 (1978), pp. 227–241.
10. Idem., p. 232.
11. Max Weber, *Politics als Beruf*, in H.H. Gerth and C. Wright Mills (Translated and edited), *Max Weber: Essays in Sociology*, pp. 77–128 (USA: Oxford University Press, 1946).
12. Ibid.
13. Roberto Mangabeira Unger, *Plasticity to Power* (London: Verso, 2004).
14. For example, as conducted in Barrington Moore, *Social Origins of Dictatorship and Democracy: Lord and Peasant in the Making of the Modern World* (USA: Beacon Press, 1993).
15. Joel Migdal, *State in Society: studying how states and Societies Transform and Constitute one Another* (USA: Cambridge University Press, 2001), p. 15.
16. Ibid., p. 47.

17. Organisation for Economic Co-operation and Development, *Supporting Statebuilding in Situations of Conflict and Fragility: Policy Guidance, DAC, Guidelines and Reference Series*, (OECD Publishing, 2011).

18. For definitions of these, see Juan Linz, *Totalitarian and Authoritarian Regimes* (USA: Lynne Rienner, 2000), p. 34.

19. Susan Strange, *The Retreat of the State. The diffusion of power in the world economy* (USA: Cambridge University Press), p. xii.

20. Jeffery Herbst, *States and Power in Africa: Comparative Lessons in Authority and Control* (USA: Princeton University Press, 2000).

21. As far as the interactions between these two sources of dysfunction goes, there is the intriguing possibility that the twin tasks of "mastering one's environment," and "developing a strong state" are linked by precisely the same kind of ratchet effect that Tilly uses to describe the growth of the European state, that is, the interlinked evolution of capital and coercion. Certainly, in early Medieval Europe the destruction of the wild, ungoverned spaces and their subsequent penetration by the forces of order produced a series of benefits for those forces; which in turn enabled them to deforest more effectively. It is this linkage between the extension of state power and the mastery of the environment which is responsible for the opprobrium associated with the English words, "pagan" and "heathen," for these words meant both an enemy of the (Christian) state, but also someone who dwelled in the wild spaces (Latin: "paganus"; English: "heath") outside society. See Felipe Fernandez-Armesto, *Civilizations* (Macmillan, 2000), pp. 137–147 and Charles Tilly, *Coercion, Capital, and European States, AD 990–1990* (USA: Blackwell Ltd., 1990).

22. William Reno, *Warlord Politics and African States* (USA: Lynne Reinner, 1998).

23. Idem., ix.

24. Idem., p. 38.

25. Quoted in Antulio J. Echevarria, II, 'On the Clausewitz of the Cold War: Reconsidering the Primacy of Policy in On War,' *Armed Forces & Society* 34; 90 (2007).

26. Mary Kaldor, *New and Old Wars: Organized Violence in a Global Era* (USA: Stanford University Press, 2007).

27. Martin van Creveld, *The Transformation of War* (USA: Free Press, 1991).

28. David Kilcullen, *Out of the Mountains: The Coming Age of the Urban Guerrilla* (USA: Cambridge University Press, 2013).

29. Assis Malaquias, 'Diamonds are a guerrilla's best friend: the impact of illicit wealth on insurgency strategy,' *Third World Quarterly* 22:3 (2001) pp. 311–325; see also US general Stanley McChrystal's assertion that "it takes a network" to fight networked insurgents (Stanley A. McChrystal, 'It Takes a Network: The New Front Line of Modern Warfare', *Foreign Policy* (March–April 2011).

30. Mark Duffield, 'War as a Network Enterprise: The New Security Terrain and its Implications,' *Cultural Values* 6:1 (2002), pp. 153–165.
31. With a few exceptions: see Dylan Craig, 'Ultima Ratio Regum: Remix or Redux?' State Security Policy and Proxy Wars in Self-Governing Africa, *Strategic Insights* 9 (2010): 3–37; also, Craig, "Developing a Comparative Perspective on the Use of Non-States in War," *Journal of African Security* 4, no. 3 (2011): 171–194.
32. Unger, *Plasticity into Power*, p. 8.
33. Stephen M. Walt, "Alliance formation and the balance of world power." *International security* 9.4 (1985): 3–43.
34. Tanisha M. Fazal, *State death: the politics and geography of conquest, occupation, and annexation* (USA: Princeton University Press, 2011).
35. For example, Correlates of War, MIDs, UCDP-PRIO, and other widely used datasets: see Paul R. Hensel, 'ISA Compendium: SSIP Data Sets', http://www.paulhensel.org/compendium.html. Accessed February 3, 2019.
36. BBC. 'Russia's border doesn't end anywhere, Vladimir Putin says,' November 24, 2016. https://www.bbc.com/news/world-europe-38093468. Accessed February 2, 2019.
37. https://www.prio.org/Data/Armed-Conflict/UCDP-PRIO/.
38. "In recent years there has been an increase in the number of intrastate conflicts that are internationalized—that is, that have another state supporting one side or another. Such involvement often has the effect of increasing casualty rates and prolonging conflicts." Stockholm International Peace Research Institute. 1. Armed Conflict. 2013. http://www.sipri.org/yearbook/2013/01. Accessed February 2, 2019.
39. H. Buhaug & J.K. Rød 'Local determinants of African civil wars, 1970–2001' *Political Geography* 25 (2006): 315–335. It bears mentioning that the geolocated data used by Buhaug and Rød were also assembled by the UCDP-PRIO project, which certainly goes a long way toward suggesting that these datasets are, in their own way, attempting to find ways around the shortcomings of the dominant conflict studies models of war.
40. Boaz Atzili & Wendy Pearlman, 'Triadic Deterrence: Coercing Strength, Beaten by Weakness', *Security Studies*, 21:2 (2012), 301–335.
41. Weber, *Politic als Beruf.*
42. Jeffrey Herbst, States and Power in Africa; see also Robert H. Jackson, *Quasi-states: Sovereignty, International Relations and the Third world* (UK: Cambridge University Press, 1990).
43. "In a landmark paper on sovereignty and territoriality, Murphy (1996) distinguishes between de jure and de facto sovereignty to make this point. This distinction, however, necessarily implies that there actually is a pure de jure sovereignty from which de facto sovereignty is a lapse or anomaly.

My claim is that de facto sovereignty is all there is." John Agnew, 'Sovereignty Regimes: Territoriality and State Authority in Contemporary World Politics,' *Annals of the Association of American Geographers*, 95(2), 2005, pp. 437–461. See also Agnew's *Globalization and Sovereignty* (USA: Rowman and Littlefield), 2009, 47–96.

44. Agnew, 'Sovereignty Regimes.' 438.
45. Ibid.
46. Ibid.
47. Idem., 443
48. Idem., 441–442.
49. Ibid.
50. Idem., 445.
51. This term is drawn from Philip Bobbitt, *The Shield of Achilles: War, peace, and the course of history.* Anchor, 2007.
52. For a fuller examination, see Hendrik Spruyt, "Institutional Selection in International Relations: State Anarchy as Order." *International Organization* 48 (1994): 527–557, and also William Manchester, *A World Lit Only by Fire: The Medieval Mind and the Renaissance-Portrait of an Age* (USA: Back Bay Books, 2009).
53. *Écorcheurs* (Fr: "skinners [of dead bodies]") were the bands of roaming fighters, bandits, and ex-soldiers who pillaged the medieval French countryside in the fourteenth and fifteenth centuries; marcher lords were warlords who were given titles to lands outside the settled boundaries of a polity on the understanding that they would pacify these areas ("the March") on behalf of the crown. For a fuller examination of the marcher phenomenon, see Peter Turchin, War and peace and war: The rise and fall of empires (USA: Penguin, 2007).
54. Agnew, 'Sovereignty Regimes'.
55. Saskia Sassen, *Territory, Authority, Rights: From Medieval to Global Assemblages* (USA: Princeton University Press, 2006).
56. In general, these moves require at least bilateral buy-in from both parties affected by a conflict if the verdict of mediation or arbitration is to be accepted; however, for an examination of a form of unilateral action by states to secure resources or avoid undesirable outcomes, see Orde Kittrie's *Lawfare: Law As a Weapon of War* (Oxford University Press, 2016).
57. Vasquez, *The War Puzzle*, p. 36.
58. Kilcullen, *Out of the mountains.*
59. Dylan Craig, "Proxy War by African States, 1950–2010," PhD Dissertation, American University, 2012.

CHAPTER 2

Interstice Openers

In this chapter, I present four cases of the opening of sovereign interstices as a form of interstate violence: the naval campaigns of the Sea Beggars (1566–1600), sponsored slave revolts in the Americas (1693–1865), the reciprocal Ethiopian and Somalian proxy wars in the Ogaden and Somaliland (1973–1991), and Russian interventions in Moldova, Georgia, Azerbaijan, and Ukraine (1990–present). In each of these cases, a sponsoring (i.e., patron) state used a partnership with a non-state actor as a means to achieve a desired military outcome within the territory of one or more rival (i.e., target) states, thereby circumventing—as discussed in the previous chapter—the geopolitical demarcations which serve to systematize interstate behavior, and whose overt violation by the use of conventional forces the sponsoring states were seeking to avoid.

Operating via non-state partners in this way provides the patron state with the benefits of military action without the systemically imposed costs of relying solely on their own forces to do so; and while the specific nature of these benefits and costs varies with historical context, two common factors—which I will refer to in this chapter and the two which follow as the "key characteristics" of each kind of interstitial war—connect them and recur across all four cases discussed here.

As a brief methodological aside before I name and define these two concepts, it is important to understand what I mean when I say that certain characteristics are "key" to understanding interstice openers (in this chapter), or to understanding the other kinds of interstitial actors discussed

© The Author(s) 2020
D. Craig, *Sovereignty, War, and the Global State*,
https://doi.org/10.1007/978-3-030-19886-2_2

in Chaps. 3 and 4. For a characteristic to count as a "key" characteristic, it must pass two tests.

First, on the level of simple empirical summary, each set of "key characteristics" is common to all the cases presented in each chapter, and thus serves as a useful set of diagnostic indices to indicate that an attempt to open (or exploit, or close) an interstice has taken place. However, this is not their only utility, because it is not enough to say "what seems true of all interstice openers?" and then to mistake that post fact observation for a true definition of the practice. For one thing, there are also a variety of other elements of interstitial war more generally (e.g., the provision of arms by the state partner) which might also be included in a list of diagnostic indices indicating the presence of interstice openers—if that were all we were interested in. A more useful criterion for identifying a key characteristic is thus its exclusivity. Arms provision is indeed important to interstice openers, but it is also important to exploiters and closers; it therefore is not exclusive to the class of phenomena that I want to delineate here.

Sovereign excludability, on the other hand, is a consistent characteristic of interstice openers but not of exploiters and closers; this makes it a good candidate for being a "key characteristic." By sovereign excludability, I mean the externality to the sovereign responsibilities of their patron exhibited by the non-state partners. Put another way: to serve their patrons effectively, the non-state actors upon which interstice-opening operations rest must be excludable, or must choose to exclude themselves, from the sovereignty protections of their patron, operating deniably and illegally until such time as the state patron elects to take one of two actions: pardon the interstice openers and elevate them to formal positions within the state, or destroy them as outlaws.

Second, for a characteristic to count as "key" it must also connect to the "how" of interstitial war, that is, it must address *how* interstitial war, in particular, has been employed by the patron state in this case in order to achieve its strategic goals. Once again, if our objective were simply to make a list of reasons *why* states have engaged interstitial war throughout history, the list would be long and might include elements which interstitial war shares with other forms of war, such as "to degrade enemy capacity to resist the political will of the sponsor" or "to head off an incipient invasion." Asking "how" (or, perhaps, "why, rather than") narrows this list considerably, because we are now concerning ourselves with what interstitial war provides to the war-seeking patron that other alternatives could or did not. As with the diagnostic indices discussed earlier, this is in part a simple matter using exclusivity as a ward against endogeneity bias.

For example, it is easy to say of all war (and all interstitial war) that it is conducted to have an ideological as well as a concrete effect, but when it comes to <u>regulative plasticity</u> we will soon see that the interstitiality of this element of interstice opening is key to both *how* it works and *why* it is desirable. This makes it a far more specific characteristic of interstice openers, and thus far more deserving of "key" status. By regulative plasticity, I mean the interstice openers' ability to ignore and/or subvert legal and moral codes (regulations) within their area of operation, and their ability to leverage this subversion both in pursuit of operational effectiveness and to provoke long-term change in these regulative conventions (law, morality, etc.).

With what I mean by a "key characteristic" established, I now turn to the first of the four cases through which the descriptive and causal dimensions of interstice-opening warfare will be showcased in this chapter: the interstice-opening pirate patriots of the sixteenth- and seventeenth-century Dutch wars of independence.

THE SEA BEGGARS

The profound effects of the Thirty Years' War (1618–1648) on sovereignty generally and European sovereignty in particular is both well established in the literature at large and discussed in the concluding chapter of this book. However, the actions of the interstice-opening naval rebels discussed in this section are drawn from a larger conflict, which not only overlaid the Thirty Years' War but also preceded it by half a century. This was the Eighty Years' War, in which the Protestant territories that would become the Netherlands, Belgium, and Luxembourg fought for independence from Habsburg Spain.

As it happens, the origins of the war bespeak an interstitial overlap of jurisdictions even before the Sea Beggars' involvement: after all, the problems of governance around which the rebels rallied were not simply the result of Philip II dictating unpopular terms surrounding taxation, religious liberty, and the monopolization of violence to a set of subjects in the Low Countries, but rather that the Low Countries already had power structures of their own, with whose operation the Spanish decrees (although backed by a preponderance of force) sometimes clashed. Thus, for example, in the Netherlands the Council of State (including William of

Orange) advised the Spanish regent closely, and tried to mitigate the del-eterious effects of many disruptive policies before these could cause wide-spread problems. It was during one of these petitionary assemblies, in April 1566, that a member of the Council referred to an unruly group of petitioners as "beggars"; the term was subsequently adopted as a badge of pride by the anti-Spanish faction more generally.

The biggest problem facing the Beggars was the extent of Spanish mili-tary and moral power defending the status quo in the Low Countries. In purely military terms, an enormous force of regular Spanish troops was garrisoned within the territory. In addition, given the fact that the reli-gious divide between Protestant and Catholic largely overlapped with the political divide between the local nobles and the governing representatives of the faraway Spanish state, in moral terms this made the pursuit of "her-etics" by the local wing of the Spanish Inquisition, also a de facto tool for fragmenting opposition to the state.

Luckily for the rebels, a variety of factions across the Low Countries could be counted on to contest the moral forces opposing Low Country home rule. Calvinist and Anabaptist zealots did just during the waves of anti-Catholic collective violence (the *Beeldenstorm*) which took place dur-ing 1566, but not all resistance took such physical form. An equally sub-versive but entirely peaceful form of protest at the time involved the minting of *geuzenpenningen*—literally, beggar's medals—displaying anti-Spanish or pro-home rule slogans. One popular medal, cast in silver in the shape of a crescent, read *Liever Turks dan Paaps* ("better to be Turkish than papist"): a bold statement indeed considering the religiously informed carnage taking place in the Mediterranean at the time, and a clear testa-ment to the Beggars' ability to provoke new and dynamic imaginings about what an independent Dutch national identity might and might not be.

Despite these ideological successes in confronting Spain's moral author-ity, no clear solution to the rebels' military disadvantage could be found to match. Attempts to raise a Protestant invasion force among Huguenot communities in France, or to use a German mercenary force to seize Brabant, were stymied by French and Spanish state counterattack respec-tively. Combined with the reprisals which followed the *Beeldenstorm*, this meant that the Beggars were overall in a worse position in 1570 than they had been before the rebellion.

There was, however, one area within the Low Countries in which Spain did not hold the upper hand: the sea. With many of the naval forces of continental Europe fighting the Ottoman Empire in the Mediterranean in the lead-up to the Battle of Lepanto in 1571, the Beggars found themselves able to combine the existing network of pirates and smugglers in the region, with the ideology of popular revolt on one hand and the certifying powers represented by letters of marque on the other, to create a de facto navy with considerable striking power. In this way, the original Beggars were, for a time at least, eclipsed by the actions of privateer captains who called themselves the "Sea Beggars" (*Watergeuzen*).

Initially operating from the French Huguenot port of La Rochelle under the sponsorship of Louis of Nassau, these maritime rebels achieved several striking successes against Spanish squadrons in the early years of the war, but their main contribution must also be seen in terms of providing the outclassed rebels with a type of warfare well suited to their current position. The Sea Beggars did not have to be raised en masse and then moved to the Low Countries through hostile territory, as had been the case in with the ill-fated Huguenot armies; nor would their willingness to fight end abruptly when they could no longer be paid in advance, as had been the case with the German mercenaries at Brabant. Instead, the Sea Beggars could disperse or concentrate as necessary in the face of enemy strength or weakness, and they would fight for a cut of future plunder rather than money up front. More importantly, they could win at a time in which rebel victories were thin on the ground.

The Sea Beggars' actions in April 1572 well exemplify this flexibility and well-suitedness to the conflict at hand. With La Rochelle under attack by French forces and English ports closed to them in an attempt to mitigate the growing tensions in the Anglo-Spanish relationship, the Sea Beggars simply doubled back to the Dutch coastline and—spontaneously operating as a land force—seized the towns of Brielle and Vlissingen, precipitating a general uprising in the province of Holland and providing the rebels with a legendary victory over the Duke of Alva which is celebrated in Dutch history and popular culture to this day.

Not long after the victory at Brielle, however, the Sea Beggars began to lose (or in some cases, were forcibly divested of) their outlaw mystique and open mandate for unrestrained action. Even the architect of the seizure of Brielle, Willem de la Marck, found himself banned from the Netherlands by order of William of Orange not two years later—possibly as a result of a massacre of Catholic priests conducted under his orders. Willem Bloys van Treslong, de la Marck's second in command, maintained a prominent position in the rebel naval forces until 1585, but even he was briefly jailed by his superiors and retired shortly thereafter. At the same time, Dutch commercial vessels bound for rebel strongholds like Utrecht found themselves increasingly menaced not just by Spanish warships but by privateers operating out of the French port of Dunkirk under Spanish license. By 1600, it was Dutch forces attacking Franco-Spanish privateer bases, rather than the other way around; during the same period, Dutch crews began to be (unsuccessfully) exhorted by their leaders to treat all privateer vessels operating from Dunkirk as pirates, and indeed to submit any captured Dunkirkers to execution by mass drowning—a practice referred to as *voetenspoelen* or "foot-wetting."

As the rebellion on land grew in scope and resilience, in other words, the Sea Beggars found that the state which had initially relied on them for its survival, now found the military and moral benefits of supporting the rebellion at sea to be outweighed by the costs of permitting its increasingly desperate enemies to do the same. This shift in priorities left the Sea Beggars facing a choice to either hang up the outlaw mantle and become a formal agent of the state, or be excluded from it.

As the cases presented in this chapter show, this moment of choice is the fundamental dilemma of the interstice opener, found not only in the stories of the Sea Beggars but also in those of the more famous English "sea dogs" such as Francis Drake, Walter Raleigh, John Hawkins, or Henry Morgan, who served the same interstice-opening role in England's Caribbean War against Spain during this era and who also found themselves either elevated or executed at the end of their careers. This points to a recurring and foundational incompatibility between interstice openers and their patrons; though the openers are in many cases critical to the survival of their patrons, the two cannot continue to exist alongside one another in perpetuity.

A broader discussion as to why, exactly, interstice openers might find themselves more welcome under the kind of sovereignty projected by a weak state or rebel proto-state (Elizabethan England, the Beggars), on one hand, and the kind of sovereignty projected by both of these entities in more stable and secure times, will be conducted in Chap. 5 when the conclusions generated by close attention to interstice exploiters (Chap. 3) and interstice closers (Chap. 4) can be added to the discussion. For now, suffice it to delineate this tension by what I will have referred to earlier as <u>sovereign excludability</u>: in other words, that to serve their patrons effectively, interstice openers must exclude themselves from the sovereignty of their patron, operating deniably and illegally until such time as the state patron elects to take one of two actions: pardon the interstice openers and elevate them to formal positions within the state, or destroy them as outlaws.

This baked-in illegality does more than simply define a shelf life for interstice openers, however; it also highlights their second key characteristic, that is, their regulative plasticity in terms being able to both opt out of or to provoke change in in the moral conventions of the areas in which they act. Regarding the former, we see in the seizure of Brielle (or, indeed, Henry Morgan's equally bold raid on Panama in 1671) that the freedom to ignore both the laws of conflict between states and the practical and operational conventions of warfare is integral to interstice-opening action, because interstice openers generally operate in conditions where deviance from moral and legal codes produces military effectiveness where it would otherwise be absent. Drake, Raleigh, and Morgan could attack unprepared Spanish targets far larger than their own forces because England and Spain were nominally at peace; the Sea Beggars could use stealth to seize fortresses that would have been far more resistant to open, formal battle, and then retreat from these prizes having extracted what they needed without engendering any loss of national prestige. In addition, and with regard to the second sense of "plasticity," this kind of interstitially flexible action often has illegality not only as its *prerequisite* but also as its *goal*.

It should thus come as no surprise to find that not only did the seizure of Brielle provoke a general uprising in Holland soon after, but also that the name "Geuzen" was reactivated by a branch of the Dutch resistance during the Nazi occupation, that the Dutch term for an unpleasant nickname that is reappropriated and taken on as an act of pride is a "beggar's name" (*geuzennaam*), or indeed that the public holiday commemorating the event in the town of Brielle ("*Kalknacht*" or "chalk night") is still associated with acts of petty vandalism and criminality today.[1] More concretely, the "Beggar's Medal Foundation" (*Stiftung Geuzenpenning*), a charity foundation established to commemorate the ideals of the initial Beggars and the World War II resistance group, awards a commemorative *geuzenpenning* each year to "to individuals or institutions that have, in some special way, devoted themselves to fighting for democracy or against dictatorship, discrimination and racism."[2] In defying law to strike at the Spanish forces, the Sea Beggars should thus be seen to have converted a few specific military successes into a general erosion of Spanish moral authority, opening so wide an interstice in the ideological landscapes of the governed that its outlines can still be seen in modern cultural memory.

I develop this idea further in the discussions of slave revolts in the Americas, and proxy irredentism in Somalia and Ukraine, next.

Sponsored Slave Revolts

Certainly, slaves have considered revolt and slave-owners have feared such revolt as long as one human has held another in bondage. However, the fears articulated in the May 29, 1776, edition of the South Carolina Gazette saw this general fear against a very specific backdrop: that of foreign sponsorship of a slave rebellion in the lead-up to the American Revolution. "There is gone down to [the docks at] Sheerness," warned the paper, "seventy-eight thousand guns and bayonets, to be sent to America, to put into the hands of N********s, the Roman Catholics, the Indians and Canadiens."[3]

As it turned out, this particular rumor was false. While the British had indeed armed Native American groups in the lead-up to the Rebellion and previously (as had the colonists), they had not contemplated arming slaves; nor was a hidden Fifth Column of Catholic insurgents poised to sweep into South Carolina with bayonets fixed. But despite its falsehood, rumors of sponsored slave revolts in the Americas did indeed have true origins, rooted over a century of slaves both in being used to further, or sometimes even inserting themselves into, the violent affairs of states. Some readers of the Gazette may have remembered the 1739 Stono Rebellion, in which a group of around 80 slaves rose in revolt, burned several plantations, and attempted to fight their way south to Spanish Florida, killing around two dozen civilians and militia in a series of clashes over the next week. Florida had been the rebels' destination for a reason: since 1693, it had been the policy of the Spanish governor of San Agustín to free any British slave that escaped into his jurisdiction. These runaways would, after converting to Catholicism, became part of a growing community of free slaves known as Fort Mose; in exchange, the community provided military service to the Spanish forces who could then leverage the spatially marginalized position of the fort and its community to gain a forward position for the Spanish defenses.

For slaves in the southern British colonies, then, and especially for Catholic Bakongo slaves such as the leaders of the Stono rebels, Fort Mose represented freedom—if they could reach it. But in terms of the model of interstitial warfare advanced in this book, it makes more sense to see Fort Mose as a hardpoint from which Spanish power could be broadcast into the sovereign interstice between San Agustín and Savannah. This interstice was beyond the direct-rule capacity of the relatively weak Spanish forces in the area, but with the right policies and careful cultivation of relationships with Native American groups and communities like the one at Fort Mose, it could serve two roles: as a buffer against British expansion, and as a steady promoter of conflict via slave revolts throughout the British plantation states. This logic appears to have been clear to the British as well, who marched on Fort Mose and destroyed it in 1740 during the War of Jenkins' Ear; although it was later rebuilt, the ceding of Spanish Florida to Britain in 1763 meant the end of its role in interstitial warfare and of its role as a place of relative freedom for its inhabitants. The free black community at the time, which included over 2000 runaway slaves, was resettled in Cuba.

Despite its apparently singular status in black history, Marx's observation about history's first repetition as tragedy applies to Fort Mose as well, for the story of its downfall was to be played out with slightly different actors not a century later, following the War of 1812. This time, the architects behind the fort's existence were British rather than Spanish; the threatened state was not a British colony but the newly constituted United States, and the fort was garrisoned not by a Spanish-led free black militia but by a mix of runaway slaves, Native Americans from the Seminole and Choctaw tribes, and Afro-Caribbean soldiers from the British Colonial Marines demobilized and allowed to retain the fort and their weapons when British forces withdrew. This fort, nameless while occupied by the British, became known as the "Negro Fort" and as with Fort Mose, became a destination for runaway slaves from as far away as Virginia.

The US government's first response to the fort's existence was to counter-fortify, beginning the construction of Fort Scott on the Florida-Georgia border nearby in order to guard the approaches to the "Negro Fort." Andrew Jackson, who had been tasked with pacifying this entire area during the First Seminole War, also issued demands that the Spanish governor of West Florida secure the area and destroy the fort, but to no avail.[4] Finally, when supply barge crews bound for the Fort Scott construction site were attacked by the fort's inhabitants, a mixed force of US Army troops and Creek warriors was sent to destroy the fort in 1816. A gunboat bombardment soon detonated the fort's powder magazine, reducing the entire site to rubble and killing all but a few of its defenders in an instant; although two leaders of the freed slave and Choctaw factions were found still alive on the site, they were executed on the spot. Between these executions and the 1818 construction of Fort Gadsden on the site of the battle, it is clear that Jackson's forces sought to definitively close the sovereign interstice opened in the area by the British in 1814, and the fact that Fort Gadsden saw no fighting from the time it was constructed until its abandonment due to a malaria outbreak in 1863, argues that in this attempt to re-knit US sovereignty in the region must be considered to have been a success.

The stories of Fort Mose and the Negro Fort might seem to suggest that all interstitial warfare by means of sponsored slave revolt ended catastrophically for the freed slaves themselves. This was not always the case. For one thing, even the states who acted so violently to close interstices in the histories recounted earlier were able, when it suited them, to work with rebel slaves. The United States had, for example, deployed the cruiser USS *General Greene* to Haiti in 1799, to provide artillery support to Toussaint L'Ouverture's forces during their assault on the city of Jacmel,[5] and although this extension of aid did little to specifically protect L'Ouverture, when combined with Spanish aid to L'Ouverture it did achieve its intended aim of incrementing the costliness and complexity of France's continued colonial presence in the West Indies. And in the British colony of Jamaica, in the very same years (1739 and 1740) as the attack on Fort Mose, the British were not only signing peace treaties with two heavily defended communities of runaway slaves, but also entering into a kind of mutual defense pact with them.

These were the Windward and Leeward Maroons,[6] two communities founded around the turn of the eighteenth century by a group of Akan or Asante people who had escaped slavery on the British sugar plantations. By 1728, British forces were assembled to find and destroy these Maroon communities, but despite six years of fighting during the First Maroon War, they were unable to achieve a decisive victory against them. The terms of the 1739 and 1740 peace accords were that Britain would grant 2500 acres to each of the Maroon communities for their unmolested use, while the Maroons would cease to aid any new runaways who escaped into their lands and, when deemed militarily necessary by the British authorities, assist in the defense of the island both against external threats and further slave revolts. In the end, only the Windward Maroons were able to parlay this treaty into long-term security against the British; when the Leeward Maroons rebelled against perceived judicial overstretch by their resident British supervisor in 1795, they were decimated during the two-year "Second Maroon War" and by a program of deportation to Nova Scotia that followed. In contrast, the Windward Maroons maintained their community's cohesion right through to Jamaica's independence, and still maintain limited sovereign independence as a self-governing indigenous community today.

What is most striking about the Maroons, though, in distinction to the communities at Fort Mose and the Negro Fort, is the power of the ideological imprint that defines their legacy. As an example of this power: Queen Nanny, the leader of the Windward Maroons during the First Maroon War against the British, occupies a prominent position in Jamaica's national historical awareness, with currency, public festivals, and even a town named after her[7]; this is the case *despite* the fact that Windward Maroon forces, in terms of their treaty with the British, played prominent roles in the battles in which several other heroes of the Jamaican struggle for freedom, such as Tacky (killed by a Maroon sharpshooter in the 1760 uprising known as "Tacky's War") and Paul Bogle (killed in the 1865 Morant Bay Rebellion), became revolutionary martyrs.[8] In the case of Queen Nanny at least, it appears that the power of her resistance against the British before 1740 is able to eclipse or crowd out the more complex and problematically counterrevolutionary elements of the Windward Maroons' subsequent history.

To conclude this discussion of the sponsored slave rebellion, we see in each case that, first, the <u>sovereign excludability</u> of slave societies located within (but apart from) the slave state itself produced both a potential site for interstitial intervention by that state's rivals and a rallying point for willing rebels; second, that this intervention could run the gamut from calls to defect aimed at destabilizing plantation economies, to the direct weaponization (i.e., training, provisioning, and military coordination) of runaway slave communities; third, that these communities could draw on a style of irregular combat well suited to life on the sovereign periphery to engage hold off colonial forces many times their size; and fourth, that complex interactions around the morality and legality of slavery rebellion (i.e., <u>regulative plasticity</u>) and collaboration necessarily preceded and followed each instance.

While the destruction and depopulation of Fort Mose and the Negro Fort have robbed contemporary onlookers of any ability to see how those communities might have looked back on their own complex legacies in subsequent years, the long history of the Maroons shows that as with the Sea Beggars, the ideological imprint of being an interstice opener runs deep.

THE OGADEN VORTEX

In 1973, Somalian president Siad Barre resumed the provision of military aid to Somali irredentist groups in Ethiopia and Kenya, thereby attempting to open and militarize a series of sovereign interstices intended to expand the Somalian state out across a "Greater Somalia" delineated in ethnonationalist terms.[9] Although Barre's actions, in hindsight, had more to do with sustaining the power dynamics which sustained his regime in Mogadishu than with any deep ethnonationalist commitment, they nonetheless provoked retaliation in kind from Ethiopia; by 1991, the reciprocal wars of interstice opening which Barre provoked had turned into a vortex of violence which destroyed both regimes. In this section, I examine these reciprocal interstice-opening wars in order to highlight the parallel roles played by <u>sovereign excludability</u> and <u>regulative plasticity</u> on either side of the battle lines.

Groups of pastoralists and *shifta* ("bandits") with more-or-less concrete ties to Mogadishu could be found in both Ethiopia and Kenya throughout the pre-colonial period.[10] The persistence of these interstitial actors into the postcolonial era can, in large part, be attributed to the haphazard delineation of the region by the British between 1945 and 1959. During this partition, several large grazing areas used by Somali nomads (such as the Haud, in Western Somalia, and the Ogaden), and several ethnically Somali regions (such as Kenya's Northern Frontier District, or NFD) were placed outside Somalian borders, thereby provoking clashes between (and the subsequent repression of) these marginal groups by Kenyan and Ethiopian authorities. From the moment of the country's independence, therefore, successive Somalian regimes responded to the plight of the rejected the legitimacy of the frontier demarcations; regaining these lost territories became a central part of the rhetorical foundations of the Somalian state. Even the five-pointed star on the Somalian flag was chosen as a reference to the five primary Somali homelands, although only three of these lay within the country's borders at the time.[11]

Supporting irredentist groups abroad had thus been an element of Somalian foreign policy ever since independence, and had been explicitly articulated by successive heads of state as an attempt to reconstitute a "Greater Somalia" adhering to pre-colonial borders. Because this essentially encouraged civil war in neighboring countries, the Greater Somalia policy led to clashes between Somali forces, their agents, and Kenyan and Ethiopian forces, especially between 1960 and 1964.[12] In the face of this explicit policy of expansion by Somalia, and the acknowledged presence of Somalian soldiers alongside the *shifta* rebels, Kenya and Ethiopia signed a mutual defense pact in 1963–1964. There can therefore be no doubt that the Kenyan and Ethiopian administrations took the Somalian claims on their land seriously, and that the Barre regime in particular (which was in power during the 1980 and 1987 renewals) constituted a plausible continuation of this threat.

In the face of this united front, the Somalian government initially allowed itself to be deterred. Barre's civilian predecessor renounced Somalia's claim on the Kenyan NFD in 1967, and concluded a durable peace treaty with the Kenyatta regime. The situation in the Ogaden failed to achieve a similar resolution, however, and by the 1970s Somalia's capacity to challenge Ethiopia militarily had changed for the better. Superpower aid was pouring into multiple sites around the Horn, but Barre had proved adept in soliciting military aid from both the United States and the USSR.[13] This aid was used to add armor, air, and naval wings to the Somali National Army (SNA), significantly closing the gap in military power between the SNA and the larger but more poorly equipped Ethiopian army.[14] At the same time, Ethiopia found itself gripped by internal strife and anti-monarchic unrest, as well as nascent rebellions in Tigray, Ogaden, and Eritrea.[15] This served to weaken the Ethiopian state and draw its forces into garrison roles across the country. In addition, US military aid—the primary source of weapons for the Selassie regime—had slowed in the face of human rights abuses conducted by the Ethiopian security forces.

In 1974, the ouster of Emperor Selassie by a group of army officers, including future head of state Haile Mengistu Miriam, provided Barre with a clear opportunity to press his claim to the largest of the contested areas on the border between the two states: the Ogaden. Two rebel groups in the area were selected to become the leading edge of the Ogaden war: the Western Somali Liberation Front (WSLF) and its ally, the Somali Abo Liberation Front (SALF), which became the primary recipients of Somalian aid in Ethiopia. Between 1974 and 1977, SNA fighters and weaponry were covertly moved across the border in support of WSLF fighters, who made steady territorial gains against the Ethiopian army as a result. The capture of the Ethiopian garrison town of Jijiga in September 1977 marked the high point of the Somalian-backed WSLF rebellion. With the fall of Jijiga, the WSLF was now in possession of 90% of the Ogaden region.

But while the WSLF made its gains in the Ogaden, in Addis Ababa the military leadership of the post-Selassie state had undergone a series of violent purges. The result of these purges was the ascendancy of the hard-line Marxist faction of Colonel Mengistu, to control of the Ethiopian state. With Mengistu's rise to power came the potential for a closer relationship between an increasingly socialist Ethiopia and the USSR; this was achieved in early 1977, and the Mengistu regime closed down the last US military base in the country (Kagnew Station, outside Asmara) in April of that year. Soviet advisors and munitions began to arrive in the country, while Soviet mediators attempted to lead the Barre and Mengistu regimes to a peace agreement and save the USSR from having to support both sides in an increasingly bloody war. Rather than lose his gains in the Ogaden, however, Barre chose to cancel Somalia's Treaty of Friendship and Cooperation with the USSR, expel his Soviet advisors, and cast aside the covert character of his involvement in the war, committing almost the entire Somalian armed forces—70,000 infantry, 600 armored vehicles, and 40 Mig-21 fighter jets—to the Ogaden.[16]

Even with these additional troops, the combined SNA/WSLF offensive faced two unexpected challenges. The first of these was a 100,000-strong militia army which the Ethiopians had raised during the rainy season, and could now deploy alongside their regular forces. The second was a 17,000-strong Cuban expeditionary force, backed by Soviet armor and artillery, which had been moved into the path of the Somalian advance. This force was deployed around the strategically significant city of Harar, where it inflicted severe casualties on the SNA and WSLF formations. Despite repeated attempts over four months, the Somalians were unable to take Harar.

By February 1978, the Ethiopians had rebuilt their own forces in the area and were able to counterattack, seizing the tactical initiative and retaking the city outskirts. With the Soviets providing airlift capabilities for the Ethiopian armed forces, the Ethiopians were also able to strike at the Somalian rear in Jijiga, recapturing the city and cutting the Somalian spearhead in half. This spelled the end for the Somalian offensive, and in the following weeks the SNA lost all the territory that it and the WSLF had captured in the previous months. In March 1978, Barre ordered the withdrawal of the last SNA unit from Ethiopian territory. Although the WSLF continued to fight, and went on to merge with other factions to form the Ogaden National Liberation Front (ONLF), it would never again make significant gains against the Ethiopians.

Despite its withdrawal from the Ogaden, the Barre administration continued to proclaim its support for the WSLF and various other irredentist militias within the Ogaden. On May Day 1978, just a few months after the last Somalian unit had left Ethiopian territory, Barre made the following declaration on Radio Mogadiscio:

> The people colonized by Abyssinia will be free. Eritrea will be free, and they cannot refuse to let them be free. Western Somalia will be free, and they cannot refuse to grant it freedom. The numerous Abo will be free because this is history, and no one can prevent the sunshine from reaching us.[17]

Barre's promise of continued support for Ethiopian irredentists was no mere public relations exercise. In January 1979, the Somalian government formally resolved to continue supporting the WSLF and ALF; indeed, support for Somali liberation groups outside the borders of the country was written into Chap. 1 of the country's draft constitution at the same set of meetings.[18] At the same time, Ethiopian military planners had begun to shift their focus from how best to defend against the Somalian incursion, to how to retaliate for it. A high-ranking member of the ruling Provisional Military Aid Committee (PMAC) had already described the Barre regime as a "reactionary enemy" who would have to be "repulsed and annihilated;"[19] in addition, Ethiopia's decision to host the anti-Barre Somali Salvation Democratic Front (SSDF) in Addis Ababa after 1979 leaves no doubt that the destruction of the Barre regime had become a strategic priority for the Ethiopians. In short order, the Ethiopian government began to foster and support anti-Barre groups. The interstitial war which the Somalian state had inaugurated was about to be turned back on it.

In February 1979, a group called the Somali Democratic Action Front (SODAF) moved its headquarters to Addis Ababa, changed its name to the Somali Salvation Front (SSF), and began operating an anti-Barre radio station beaming into Somalia (Radio Kulmis, later known as Radio Halgan[20]). The SSF leadership was dominated by Barre's political rivals: it contained exiled members of the Barre administration (ex-Minister of Justice Osman Nur Ali), close relatives of the previous head of state (Mustafa Hadji Nuur), and members of the Majertain clan who had been held responsible for a failed coup against Barre in 1978 (Colonel Ahmed Abdullahi Yusuf). By 1981, the SSF was claiming responsibility for attacks and bombings in Somalia.

The Ethiopians were also able to establish links with a second anti-Barre group, the Somali National Movement (SNM), led by exiled Somalian diplomat Hassan Adan Wadadi. At its launch in London in April 1981, the SNM articulated a clearly revolutionary agenda for Somalia, including the removal of Barre as head of state. By 1982, the SNM had entered into "productive" talks with the Ethiopian government about establishing bases for an anti-Barre insurgency in the Ogaden; around the same time, the SSF had joined with two smaller groups to form the Somali Democratic Salvation Front (SDSF). By 1982, both Radio Halgan and the Somalian government were reporting heavy fighting in the north-western regions of the country, between the SNA and SDSF guerillas supported by Ethiopian troops. The Somalians also accused the Ethiopian air force of bombing several towns in Somalia during this time.

While the SNM and SDSF constituted the most visible source of opposition to the Barre administration, the number of disaffected Somalis ready to join such subversive or revolutionary groups had been growing steadily since the outbreak of war in the Ogaden. Indeed, Somalia experienced a string of mutinies and protests during the 1980s, many of which were put down with deadly violence. This climate of tension can in part be attributed to Barre's contentious interactions with Somalia's pervasive clan and sub-clan system—a system which would display increasing salience as the unified Somalian state began to give way to a cluster of clan-dominated political groups competing for primacy and access to key parts of the national infrastructure.

By 1990, Mogadishu was an isolated city, wracked by protests and surrounded by anti-government United Somali Congress (USC) forces. On December 31 of that year, Barre fled the city, leaving Somalia without a head of state. Initial attempts to restore government under a coalition government failed when the USC expelled the rival Somali Patriotic Movement (SPM) from Mogadishu in February 1990; other factions, such as the Somali National Front (SNF), attempted to break through the USC cordon, to no avail. Then in 1991, the USC itself split along sub-clan lines, with the Habr Gedr Hawiya backing a faction led by Mohamed Farah Aideed and the Abgal Hawiya backing his rival, transitional head of state Ali Mahdi Mohammed. Militias from the two factions battled over control of Mogadishu, paralyzing the flow of international food aid and further exacerbating the poor conditions in the refugee camps which now dominated the Somalian landscape.

With Mogadishu devastated by ongoing fighting between Aideed and Ali Mahdi, and the country as a whole unable to unify under a single faction let alone a coalition government, Somalia entered a phase of near-complete internal anarchy, from which it would not emerge for 15 years.

Although Barre fell first, in Ethiopia the Mengistu regime would soon follow. Opposition to the central government from various quarters had been on the rise since the mid-1970s, with the war in the Ogaden constituting only one theater of a broader struggle by the Selassie (and later, Mengistu) regimes to maintain Ethiopian state in the face of multiple breakaway factions. This opposition began as a series of unrelated regional resistances in the northern provinces of Tigray and Eritrea. By 1976, the Ethiopian government had switched from trying to negotiate with these disparate rebels, to confronting them directly—a military strategy made possible by increasing amounts of Soviet and Cuban military aid provided to by Mengistu.

Despite initial successes by the Ethiopian armed forces in taking control of towns and other central points, the insurgents in Eritrea and Tigray continued to conduct hit-and-run operations in the countryside. Between 1978 and 1985, the Ethiopians made repeated but unsuccessful attempts to secure a decisive victory against the rebels. Each offensive by the Ethiopian armed forces resulted either in modest but costly gains (as the rebels withdrew after inflicting severe losses, as in the fighting around Nakfa in 1980), or in outright losses (as in the loss of Barentu to the rebels in 1984).

Worse still, the disparate rebel groups had now begun to coordinate their campaigns against the Ethiopian armed forces; so, for example, although Eritrean rebel groups were responsible for the bulk of the fighting during this phase of the war, the less-well-armed Tigrayan groups nonetheless kept large portions of the Ethiopian armed forces committed to a counterinsurgency campaign, thereby preventing their deployment elsewhere. The 1984–1985 famine in Ethiopia further exacerbated the problems of the Mengistu regime, not only because of the public relations fallout resulting from the charges that he was obstructing food aid to the north in order to starve out the insurgents, but also because significant amounts of NGO-raised monetary aid, intended to purchase foodstuffs, were in fact being channeled to rebel groups instead. One Tigrayan rebel leader estimated the total value of aid funds redirected funds to arms purchases during this period at $95 million.

By February 1991, the Ethiopian forces had been displaced from all but one of their coastal strongholds, and rebel artillery and light naval units were attacking and burning Ethiopia-bound cargo ships in the vicinity of the Dahlak archipelago. Attempts to retake the coast failed, and the Ethiopian armed forces' Second Army deployed for this task was subsequently encircled and destroyed. The various rebel factions were now operating in close cooperation, with armored units from the broad-based Ethiopian People's Revolutionary Democratic Front (EPRDF) backing up a Tigrayan assault in the Shewa and Gojam regions. This offensive, named "Operation Teodoros," broke through the northernmost lines of the Ethiopian armed forces at Lake Tana, while the main rebel assault (spearheaded by the EPRDF) captured the government strongholds at Welega and Nekemte in the west. By mid-May, the rebel forces were just 300 km from the capital; two weeks later, rebel troops entered Addis Ababa, overthrowing the remnants of the Derg and bringing the civil war to an end.

In the cases already discussed in this chapter, I have showed how sovereign excludability and regulative plasticity play crucial roles in the operations of interstice-opening actors. In this regard the series of interlinked conflicts that I have referred to here as the "Ogaden Vortex" is no exception.

At first glance, however, the extent of the sovereign excludability of some of the interstitial actors involved in the Ogaden Vortex seems uneven. As Somali diaspora groups resident in Ethiopia, the SNM and SDSF were indeed external to and thus excludable from the sovereign responsibilities of their patron, requiring only to be pointed in the direction of the Barre regime and allowed to further the Mengistu regime's goals through the simple pursuit of their own. Not only this but, despite having essentially created these entities, Ethiopia would not explicitly refer to them as "sovereign states" until almost 30 years later, and even then only after it had become clear that their place in a reconstituted Somalia would be as disparate elements of a weakly bound federal state rather than as contenders for power in a unified Somalia that might one day revive pan-Somali nationalism in the Ogaden.[21]

For the WSLF and its allies, however, the excludability is less immediately clear. After all, were each of these groups not directly claimed as partners in the pan-ethnic "Greater Somalia" project by the Barre government, thereby representing a powerful emphasis on sovereign *includability* rather than excludability? The way forward in this regard is to examine not only the moment at which this partnership was explicitly established but also the moment in which it was (far more covertly) dissolved. The WSLF are properly considered to be "excludable" in terms of Somalian sovereignty because, when it suited the Somalian state to promise to withdraw from the interstitial war it had created in the Ogaden, it could hold to the letter of its promise by withdrawing its formal agents (the SNA) while leaving the WSLF as a stay-behind force. The irredentist cause of the WSLF fighters in the Ogaden, and indeed of the similarly abandoned Somali groups in the Kenyan NFD, could thus be included in the Somalian state, or not, as the moment demanded; and this is indeed the kind of excludability which interstitial actors bring to a partnership with a state actor.[22]

In terms of <u>regulative plasticity</u>, the second key characteristic of use of interstice-opening actors, the Ogaden Vortex provides three striking parallels. First, both Somalia and Ethiopia entered the conflict with pronounced vulnerabilities to internal challenges to the state's moral and legal authority, resulting from incomplete nation-building projects. In Ethiopia, these vulnerabilities were geopolitical in origin and arose from the state's origins as a tribute-extracting highland empire surrounded by subservient polities; in Somalia, they were the result of Siad Barre's incomplete (and, one might argue, deliberately bad-faith) efforts to delink clan politics from state institutions under his policy of "Scientific Socialism." Second, both states directly targeted these vulnerabilities in their provision of aid to rebel factions such as the SNM and WSLF, delegitimizing their rival's regime at its source (as being either "colonialist" or "reactionary") and using available media channels (such as radio) to ensure that this delegitimizing message was broadly disseminated. Third, both states experienced a sustained collapse of governance which outlasted the actual period during which their rivals were destabilizing them, as in both cases the military and moral damage inflicted on each regime by the interstitial agents of its rival continued to self-perpetuate and draw fresh factions and rebel groups into the fight. Proximity to the Ogaden Vortex, in other words, not only required that the sponsoring states select interstitial partners with sufficient regulative plasticity to rebel against their governments, but also produced a cascade of regulative plasticity on both sides of the contested border large enough to destroy both regimes: interstitial war in a "fire and forget" configuration.[23]

THE LITTLE GREEN MEN

In the previous chapter, I advanced the idea that recognizing interstitial war as a phenomenon with considerable historical precedent, rather than as some *sui generis* element of the modern conflict landscape, would permit inroads into otherwise opaque contemporary conflicts. It is therefore fitting that the final case to be discussed in this chapter on war by interstice opening is a connected series of contemporary conflicts noted for their opacity: the post-Cold War Russian interventions in Moldova, Georgia, Azerbaijan, and (particularly) Ukraine. Seen through the conventional international relations lenses discussed in Chap. 1, it is very hard indeed to classify these four conflicts—are they Russian regional peacekeeping missions, Moscow-backed irredentist conflicts, or a soft invasion by Russian regular forces concealing their identity behind the generic green uniforms which have led Ukrainians to refer to them as "little green men" (*zelonyye lyudishki*)?[24] In terms of the interstitial war model, though, these multiple Russian initiatives have a great deal in common, and delineate a clear policy of using interstice opening not so much to achieve regional territorial goals as global strategic ones. I explore these goals later, alongside a brief discussion of the status of the "open secret" nature of sovereign excludability in contemporary interstitial warfare, in order to bring our sense of the utility and the constituencies of operation exhibited by interstice openers up to the current day.

In terms of coercive acts of foreign policy, Russia has provided no shortage of grist for the security studies mill in recent years. Stephen Blank writes:

> In 2014 alone, Moscow repeatedly threatened the Baltic and Nordic states and civilian airliners, heightened intelligence penetration, deployed unprecedented military forces against those states, intensified overflights and submarine reconnaissance, mobilized nuclear forces and threats, deployed nuclear-capable forces in Kaliningrad, menaced Moldova, and openly violated the Intermediate-Range Nuclear Forces Treaty of 1987. Russian officials openly declared that the Conventional Forces in Europe Treaty of 1989 was dead, and continued a large-scale comprehensive defense buildup in areas ranging from space and counter-space to submarine and ground forces as well as nuclear forces.[25]

Two possibilities obtain in terms of making sense of these acts. First, it may be that Russia is using these acts to defend or expand a buffer zone against its rivals, that is, a neo-Iron Curtain behind which it enjoys de facto sovereignty through the exercise of various forms of "forward policy."[26] Second, Russia may instead be using these incidents to advance, through the repeated opening of sovereign interstices, a far more subtle global agenda.

To address the first of these options, it is clear that if Russia is defending a "backyard," it should be possible within the social science approach to determine where this backyard is. However, this task is more complex than it seems. Tempting as it might be to assume that the map of these incidents and the map of which parts of the globe Russia considers to be its geopolitical "backyard" or intervention zone are coeval, to make such an assertion would be to fall prey to endogenous thinking. As just one example, there exists the strong possibility that many states into which Russia has not yet projected some form of menacing power are nonetheless states into which it would intrude if some set of interests were threatened. Indeed, part of the political theater of current Russian forward policy is to allow states like Estonia, Latvia, and Lithuania to torment themselves with the possibility that they are in Russia's "intervention zone" even though no concrete moves have yet been made against them.[27] At the same time, Russia has engaged in forward policy against some states (such as Norway) for which the prospect of a Georgian-style intervention seems remote.

A more methodical way of identifying Russia's intervention zone is to develop five different configurations, or images, of the Russian sovereign interstice, ranging from the most to the least expansive—in other words, five configurations which describe a larger and larger area within which Russia has interests that might provoke intervention, but where it is legally unable to directly deploy formal state forces. From smallest to largest, these potential interstitial zone images are:

- All states that share a land border with Russia (12 states)
- All states that, along with Russia, made up the old USSR (14 states)
- All countries that, along with Russia, made up of the Council for Mutual Economic Assistance (COMECON) and Warsaw Pact alliances (26 states)
- All ex-USSR member states, plus all states bordering them (27 states)
- All states bordering Russia, as well all states bordering those states (46 states)

These five images of what a Russian intervention zone might look like run, roughly, from least to most expansionist; or from more to less globally revisionist. Thus, the smaller the image we can identify as having the best explanatory fit to the interventionist phenomena of Russian forward policy, the more status we should accord the idea that Russia's image as a global revisionist is based on irrational cultural memories of the Cold War; on the other hand, the larger the image that is required the more merit we should assign to the idea that Russia is indeed a "breed apart" from other "large middle" powers.

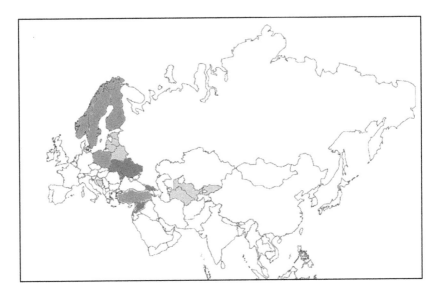

Fig. 2.1 Sites of Russian intervention, 1990–2018

Figure 2.1 depicts a sampling of Russian forward policy incidents since 1990:

In this map, "economic warfare" such as sanctions or military assistance to a rival power is indicated as yellow; opportunistic and restricted military deployments (such as airspace and maritime boundary violations, or troop buildups in Kaliningrad) are indicated with orange; and actual deployment of Russian troops either in "open secret" or as "peacekeepers" is marked in red.

An immediate challenge to the simple ascription of these events to any of the five configurations of Russia's intervention zone is immediately apparent. For one thing, countries such as Sweden and Turkey, which have experienced Russian "forward policy" of a more-than-accidental kind, only appear in two of the five images outlined above; and yet, were those two images indeed a useful map of where Russia is disposed to intervene through interstitial war, we would also expect intensified use of aggressive forward policy in southeast Asia, the South Caucasus, and Western Europe.

At the same time, the intensity of Russian forward policy does not show a clear and uncomplicated relationship to direct proximity. Georgia and the Ukraine, as Russian neighbors, have indeed faced with direct military threat across their borders with Russia while Azerbaijan, Uzbekistan, Kyrgyzstan, and Turkmenistan have faced the kinds of Russian power projection which are easier to deploy at range; however, this correlation between contiguity and the experience of violence is inverted for the Baltic States (which should have been militarily menaced as Sweden and Turkey were, if proximity was all that mattered) and for Moldova (which should not have been invaded if proximity was a powerful factor).

Table 2.1 represents this mismatch by treating the number of intervention zone images in which a given state appears as a rough measure of the increasing likelihood that it is indeed a site which Russia considers proximal or more attractive for interstitial intervention. Against this is set an actual account of Russian forward policy events since 1990, showing that proximity and intervention are partially but not entirely covariant.

Table 2.1 Number of intervention zone images as a measure of likelihood that Russia considers intervention

Country clusters, ranked by decreasing proximity	Forward policy events
Seven "highest proximity" countries: Azerbaijan, Belarus, Estonia, Georgia, Kazakhstan, Latvia, Ukraine (appear in all five potential intervention zones images sketched above)	Three deployments of ground troops, three instances of economic coercion
Ten "high proximity" countries: Armenia, Kyrgyzstan, Lithuania, Moldova, Mongolia, North Korea, Norway, Tajikistan, Turkmenistan, Uzbekistan (appear in four potential intervention zone images)	Four instances of economic coercion (Kyrgyzstan, Lithuania, Turkmenistan, Uzbekistan), one instance of border violation (Norway), one deployment of ground troops (Moldova)
Seven "medium proximity" countries: China, Czech Republic, Finland, Hungary, Poland, Romania, Slovakia (appear in three potential intervention zone images)	Two instances of border violations (Finland and Poland)
Seven "low proximity" countries: Afghanistan, Albania, Bulgaria, Germany, Iran, Turkey, Vietnam (appear in two potential intervention zone images)	No coercive events noted
Fifteen "lowest proximity" countries: Bangladesh, Bhutan, Bosnia and Herzegovina, Croatia, India, Kosovo, Laos, Macedonia, Myanmar, Nepal, Pakistan, Serbia, Slovenia, South Korea, Sweden (appear in only one potential interventional zone image)	One count of economic coercion (Bosnia and Herzegovina), one instance of border violation (Sweden)

It is therefore clear that none of the images introduced previously can entirely account for extant incidents of Russian forward policy, or for their intensity. Why might this be the case? Two interlinked possibilities obtain. First, both the core presumption of the model being used (i.e., that Russia has a "zone" within which it seeks to preserve Russian influence through interstitial action) and the data itself (i.e., the list of forward policy incidents) require further calibration and refinement before the specific score assigned to any given country can necessarily be taken at face value. It may be, for example, that Russia's intervention zone is primarily composed of those countries with a substantial Russian minority population, or of those countries on which Russia's energy export industry relies, or those countries considering NATO (North Atlantic Treaty Organization) membership. Producing a sixth, seventh, and eighth "intervention zone image" to represent these theoretical positions, however, might only serve to throw good analytic effort after bad; this is because regardless of what "key factor" each theory selects, each is in that moment making the assumption that Russia, as a geopolitical actor, has a static set of preferences and a crude, non-strategic algorithm for selecting foreign policy (e.g., "always act to defend Russian pipelines"). But what if this is *not* the case?

One simple way that this assumption might be false is if Russian forward policy has less to do with the location or characteristics of the state being intervened in, and more to do with inflicting a maximally exhausting series of defeats on Putin's foreign opponents at a global level, that is, regardless of the site in which these contests take place. This returns us to the second possible explanation for Russian interventionism introduced earlier, that is, that Russia is not defending a buffer zone as much as fighting a global war for hierarchical primacy and using interstice opening to do so.

Multiple authors have already focused on this idea as a way of understanding whether Russia's regional foreign policy actions constitute a form of strategic signaling on a global level rather than a regional one. The consensus within such examinations is that for Russia, global geostrategic risks currently outweigh geopolitical rewards, and that the only sensible way forward is to seek a series of asymmetric contests in which small, low-risk victories can be achieved while avoiding any actual escalation into direct confrontation. Lawrence Freedman, for example, addresses Vladimir Putin's famous assertion, "If I wanted … in two days I could have Russian troops not only in Kiev, but also in Riga, Vilnius, Tallinn, Warsaw, and Bucharest,"[28] as follows:

The readiness to suggest unlimited ambition and the ability to project power well beyond its borders fits in with a Russian strategy geared to intimidation and deterrence. Yet Russia's capacity is limited. It rebuilt its armed forces during recent years of economic growth, but it would struggle to cope with a multi-front campaign or a prolonged occupation of a substantial hostile population. Should any action trigger NATO's Article V commitments, Russian forces would be outnumbered and face superior air power from the US and other allies.[29]

The notion of Russia as a kind of bluster-filled margin trader is apparent not only in positions such as Freedman's but also in work that has been done on Russia's own formulations of its strategic doctrine. Andrew Monaghan, examining the Strategy 2010 and 2020 documents, portrays Russia as an actor with a very clear idea of its difficult surroundings and a cautious plan to chart a path through these,[30] while Stephen Cimbala casts Putin as a latter-day Sun Tzu, adept in the use of flexible military persuasion as a substitute for actual (and risky) deployments of force:

Vladimir Putin took Crimea not only by force but also by successful use of military persuasion. He played chess against his opponents inside and outside of Ukraine, including the United States and NATO, in order to limit the impact of Ukraine's ouster of the Russia-friendly Yanukovych government and to keep his hand in the negotiations about post-Yanukovych Ukraine, under the brooding omnipresence of Russian military power ever close by. Putin maneuvered his opponents into a situation in which they would have to escalate dramatically in order to reverse his coup in Crimea in a timely manner, and Western governments lacked both the resolve and the capability to do so.[31]

In assessing the utility of the loss-avoidance perspective to a predictive model of Russian forward policy, we see the potential for a model that can handle variance and produce a hypothesis-like statement. Specifically, if indeed Russia were using the "little green men" as one part of a globally ambitious but extremely loss-averse strategy, this could be stated as a three-step strategic algorithm:

1. Build and maintain Russian influence through bilateral and multilateral coalition-building
2. Oppose any attempts to extend opponent influence into Russian sphere of interest
3. Take opportunistic and limited actions at opponent's expense when possible

Returning, via this algorithm, to the "little green men" with which we began our examination of Russian policy after 1990, we find substantial evidence in favor of the idea that Russia acts not only through deploying little green men, along its borders, but also by designing and maintaining integrative institutions that connect it to states across the continent and indeed the world. Given this, we might at least entertain the notion of Russia as the center of a "Greater Europe from Lisbon to Vladivostok"—a concept first advanced by Putin himself in 2010.[32]

Presumably, such a union would have as its core scaffolding a series of regional trade organizations (RTOs) and collective security organizations in the rough mold of NATO and the EU; and Russia has indeed made substantial progress in replacing the defunct Soviet-era COMECON and Warsaw Pact with more modern integrative apparatus. One version of the notion that a key motivator and technique for Russian forward policy is institutional integration, therefore, concerns itself primarily with detailing these apparatus:

> Over the past decade, Russia has created new economic and collective security organizations—most notably, the Eurasian Economic Community (EurAsEC) and the Collective Security Treaty Organization (CSTO) … [m]eanwhile, in 2001, Georgia, Ukraine, Azerbaijan, Moldova, and Uzbekistan (which later withdrew) created the GUAM Organization for Democracy and Economic Development … [w]hat makes the development of these international economic and collective security organizations especially interesting … is the differentiation that has occurred between those associated with Russia in CSTO and EurAsEC and those which are not members of CSTO and participate in GUAM and the EU's [competing] Eastern Partnership. That differentiation raises the question of whether, and if so to what extent, the creation of CSTO and EurAsEC provides additional modes of potential leverage for Russia vis-à-vis the other post-Soviet states— leverage which, in the case of its partners in CSTO and EurAsEC, may dampen any enthusiasm they might otherwise have for strengthening democratic elements in their polities and, in the case of the states participating in GUAM and the Eastern Partnership, may subject them to pressure when policy preferences consistent with their stated objectives of strengthening democracy and deepening their ties with the EU clash with those of Russia.[33]

Although Cameron and Orenstein hold EurAsEC, CSTO, and GUAM to be the primary crucibles for Russian integrative experiments in the region, it bears mentioning that they are neither the only such liberal organizations in the region, nor the last word in Russian innovation. The

Shanghai Cooperation Treaty, established between China, Kazakhstan, Kyrgyzstan, Russia, Tajikistan, and Uzbekistan in 2001, admitted India and Pakistan as members in 2017[34]; at the same time, the post-Soviet Commonwealth of Independent States is still extant, although its internal politics are far more fractious than those of the more recently formed RTOs. Indeed, Russia is an active participant in integrative multilateral organizations all across Eurasia,[35] and thus in one sense we can draw our vision of what a "Greater Europe" might look like not from the Kremlin but from the Hague—a "USS-EU." On the other hand, Russian policy has at times shrunk its stated interests to the slightly smaller area of interest comprised of Russia proper, plus all areas inhabited by ethnic Russians. This more culturally specified version of a "Greater Europe" has a tighter internal logic and a far more exclusive membership:

> Russia does not share Western interests. In [internal] documents, the Kremlin sees American influence and NATO as a threat, pledges to defend the interests of Russians wherever they live, and claims privileged interests and rights in regions adjacent to Russia. Bugajski also brings our attention to a January 2012 *Nezavisimaya Gazeta* article authored by Putin, wherein the Russian president lays out a broad and ambitious vision for a new, multiethnic Russian empire based on "Russian values."[36]

Regardless of which of these two visions is more correct, a plausible role for the little green men and the indispensability of sovereign excludability and regulative plasticity to their operations can now finally be advanced: they are the tool with which the Russian state and the Putin regime creates the uncertainty that integration into the various "Greater Europe" projects are designed to protect against. The little green men, after all, do not actually invade the states in which they appear, and while Russia is quick to dissolve de facto boundaries between the territories occupied in this manner, it specifically stops short of formally seeking to add them to Russia or to assert that it controls them. In the quasi-sovereign enclaves of Abkazia and South Ossetia in Georgia, for example, Russia has specifically disavowed the notion that its forces are anything other than peacekeepers defending a pair of independent states[37]—albeit that these "independent states" are not recognized by the broad international community and are thus entirely dependent on Russia for aid and trade.

The Georgian experience—conflict-ridden secessionist territories stuck halfway between Russian vassalhood and actual independence—plays out wherever the little green men are found, from Transnistria in Moldova to Donbass in Ukraine; and this, I would argue is the very point and the reason that interstice-opening instruments (the little green men) have been used at all. Were the little green men not possessed of <u>sovereign excludability</u>, Russia would be forced to define its relationship to the areas it invaded: but because they are excludable, an "open secret" which everyone knows represent the Russian military but which Russia ostensibly disavows, they can instead propagate a kind of useful indeterminacy, a de jure ambiguity which facilitates rather than hinders Russia's de facto control of these regions.

The utility of ambiguity also explains the key role played by <u>regulative plasticity</u> in the Russian strategy. In deploying the little green men while disavowing them, the Putin regime catches onlookers in the scholarly, journalistic, and military communities between two contradictory signals, one aggressive and one conciliatory; one honest and one a lie, one overt and one covert. This moral paradox seemingly defies or confuses conventional analysis; the result has been a flurry of alarmist thinkpieces and contradictory assertions about Russian "intentions," largely inspired or situated against amateur psychological profiles of Vladimir Putin—what we might term "Putinomania."[38] We are told, for example, that Putin exhibits a "blend of audacity and mendacity" while attempting to "convince the world community that up is down and black is white"[39]; that we will understand his foreign policy if only we understand chess[40] or perhaps judo, with its reliance on "immediate tactics, not long-term strategy"[41]; that Putin's foreign policy is driven such personal anger that there is "one comparison still cannot be overlooked in addressing Putin's vindictiveness, and that is to Joseph Stalin"[42]; and finally, that the sum of all these factors must be the realization that Putin's aim is that of "war with the West."[43]

My aim in this conclusion is not to definitively assert that any of these individual theses are untrue. Rather, I include them here to show how little progress they allow us to make if our intention is to derive from them a singular Russian plan for the maintenance of a singular and geographically distinct Russian "backyard." Instead, I would argue, the backyard is global; and the plan is ambiguous because ambiguity is the plan. For such a policy, one tool is perfectly suited to the needs of the Putin regime: interstice opening via the little green men. Their story thus provides a useful capstone to the discussion of the utility of interstice opening as a tool of war conducted in this chapter.

CONCLUSION

Table 2.2 shows a summary of the cases discussed in this chapter and the significance of the roles played by sovereign excludability and regulative plasticity in each case.

As can be seen in Table 2.2, substantial parallels connect the interstice-opening cases profiled in this chapter. All of the interstitial actors in question were able to leverage their externality to the sovereign responsibilities of their patron, and their ability to ignore and/or subvert legal and moral

Table 2.2 Summary of cases involved in interstitial opening

Case	Sovereign excludability	Regulative plasticity
The Sea Beggars (1566–1600)	The Beggar fleets represented Low Country interests but their dual nature as both pirates and self-financing naval units allowed them to strike at the weakest part of the Spanish occupation and circumvent state-level initiatives like the closure of the English ports	Sea Beggar victories eroded the moral authority of the Spanish authorities and served both to inspire general uprisings and to widen (via the slogan *Liewer Turks dan Paaps*) the horizons of the pursuit of an independent national identity
Slave revolts (1693–1865)	Slaves' dual positioning, both within the economic systems and outside the political systems of slave societies in the Americas provided rival states with a ready-made site for economic warfare and a readily mobilizable population of willing defectors specialized in interstitial defense	The promise of manumission or quasi-sovereign self-rule not only served to galvanize slave rebellions, but also provoked slave societies to take drastic and wasteful measures to shut down slave escape routes, and provided a rallying point capable of obscuring problematic histories of collaboration.
The Ogaden Vortex (1973–1991)	The use of proxy forces allowed the Barre and Mengistu regimes to sign peace treaties while still pursuing wars of extermination against one another	The unstable national coalitions of Cold War era Somalia and Ethiopia proved highly susceptible to the erosion of moral authority provoked by sponsored irredentist violence
Little green men (1990–present)	Russian soft interventions serve to paralyze international response and produce a series of vassal quasi-states whose ambiguous status under international law permits continued Russian military occupation	Contradictory messaging surrounding Russian intentions serves as a threat multiplier and provides a coercive flip side to Russian alliance politics throughout Eurasia

codes (regulations) within their area of operation, to weave military victory into moral victory and vice versa.

Beyond these parallels, the stories of the interstice openers presented also serve to provide the first validation of this book's cross-historical scope. Indeed, while a twenty-first-century reader may think that it was the image-conscious liberal democracies of the post-World War II world that first saw the need for deniable military action, conducted by small specialized teams behind enemy lines and undertaken with the reception of their actions as a key consideration, we see as far back as the Sea Beggars that this approach to combining military and moral goals through interstitial action has a far wider appeal. We also see in the more contemporary cases of Ogaden and Eastern Europe, the deleterious regulative effects that await sovereign entities that ignore or fail to contain interstice-opening acts of violence.

Notes

1. Wereld Feesten Almanak. Kalknacht. 2019. https://www.beleven.org/feest/kalknacht. Accessed January 30, 2019.
2. Stichting Geuzenverzet 1940–1945. 2007. https://www.geuzenpenning.nl/index.php?tekst_id=4&lang=EN. Accessed January 30, 2019.
3. Raphael, A People's History of the American Revolution, p. 312.
4. Jackson's letter reads, in part, as follows: "Sir, I am charged by my government to make known to you that a Negroe Fort, erected during our late war with Britain … has been strengthened since that period, and is now occupied by upwards of two hundred and fifty negroes, many of whom have been enticed away from the service of their Masters, Citizens of the United States, [and] all of which are well armed clothed and disciplined … *[secret] practices to inveigle Negroes from the frontier citizens of Georgia as well as from the Cherokee and Creek nations … are still continued by this Banditti …* [the] principles of good faith which always insure good neighborhood between Nations require the immediate and prompt interference of the Spanish Authority; to destroy or remove from out frontier this Banditti, to put an end to an evil of so serious a nature, and return to our citizens and the friendly Indians inhabiting our Territory those Negroes now in the fort which have been stolen and enticed from them … this Banditti's conduct will not be tolerated by our government and if not put down by the Spanish authority will compel us in self Defence to destroy them." [emphasis added]. Quoted in Harold D. Moser, David R. Hoth,

George H. Hoemann, *The Papers of Andrew Jackson: Volume IV, 1816–1820* (University of Tennessee Press, 1994), pp. 22–23.

5. Cyril James, *The Black Jacobins; Toussaint L'Ouverture and the San Domingo Revolution* (USA: Vintage Books, 1963), p. 91.

6. Maroon, from the Spanish *cimarron* meaning "wild" or "untamed," was a term coined by Europeans in the Americas to describe slaves living in communities out of easy reach of the authorities. Windward and Leeward refer to the eastern and western sides of the island respectively.

7. E. Hartman Reckord, 'October 19 Is Nanny Day in Moore Town, Portland', Jamaica Information Service (October 19, 2015). https://jis.gov.jm/october-19-is-nanny-day-in-moore-town-portland/. Accessed February 3, 2019.

8. Michael Sivapragasam, *After the treaties: a social, economic and demographic history of Maroon society in Jamaica, 1739–1842*. University of Southampton, Doctoral Thesis, 2018.

9. Emmanuel N. Amadife and James W. Warhola. Africa's Political Boundaries: Colonial Cartography, the OAU, and the Advisability of Ethno-National Adjustment. *International Journal of Politics, Culture, and Society*, Vol. 6, No. 4 (Summer, 1993), pp. 533–554.

10. Donald Crummey, *Banditry, Rebellion, & Social Protest in Africa* (UK: Heinemann, 1986), pp. 133–140.

11. Somali poet Xaaji Aadan (1914–2005) described the importance of the Somalian flag in the following terms: *Afriiqiyada Bari buu u yahay shamis arooryaade / Sida qamarka oogada jiruu ugu iftiimaaye / Ummaddii la googooyey buu ururinaayaaye* ("For all of East Africa, the Somali flag rises like the sun, and shows the way ahead like the moon. **The flag will unite what the colonists have divided**." [emphasis added]. For further analysis, and the full text of the poem, see Ali H. Abdulla, 'A new Club for Somalia based on the Vision of Xaaji Aadan Af-Qallooc,' WardheerNews. com, July 5, 2009. https://www.somalinet.com/forums/viewtopic.php?t=217274#p2499753. Accessed February 3, 2019.

12. Metz, H. C., Library Of Congress. Federal Research Division & Thomas Leiper Kane Collection. (1993) Somalia: A Country Study. Washington, DC: Federal Research Division, Library of Congress: For sale by the Supt. of Docs., U.S. G.P.O. [Pdf] Retrieved from the Library of Congress, https://www.loc.gov/item/93016246/. Accessed February 3, 2019.

13. The primary factor underlying this aid flow was the geopolitical salience of the Red Sea region, which not only lay alongside the oil fields of the Middle East, but also the strategically vital Suez Canal trade route.

14. John Turner, *A Continent Ablaze: The Insurgency Wars in Africa, 1960 to the Present*. (South Africa: Jonathan Ball Publishing, 1998).

15. John Markakis, 'Nationalities and the State in Ethiopia', *Third world quarterly*, 11:4, Ethnicity in World Politics (Oct, 1989), pp. 118–130.
16. Gebru Tareke, "The Ethiopia-Somalia War of 1977 Revisited," *International Journal of African Historical Studies*, 2000 (33), p. 648.
17. Ioan M. Lewis, *A Modern History of Somalia* (UK: Longman, 1980).
18. Keesing's Record of World Events (formerly Keesing's Contemporary Archives), Volume XXIV, May, 1978 'Ethiopia, Ethiopian', Page 29706.
19. Keesing's Record of World Events, Volume XXIV, May, 1978 'Ethiopia, Ethiopian', Page 28989.
20. "Kulmis" meaning "Unity." The station was renamed Radio Halgan ("Struggle") in 1982. See also Canada: Immigration and Refugee Board of Canada, Somalia: Information regarding Radio Kulmis, 1 May 1990, SOM5487, available at: https://www.refworld.org/docid/3ae6ab2448.html [accessed January 21, 2019].
21. Afrol News. 2019. 'Somaliland closer to recognition by Ethiopia. http://www.afrol.com/articles/25633. Accessed January 30, 2019; also, Robert Draper, 'Shattered Somalia', *National Geographic* 216:3 (September 2009), pp. 70–97.
22. The take-or-leave flexibility of interstitial clan actors in the Ogaden is to be contrasted with Barre's disastrous attempts to exclude some clans from access to neopatrimonial power sources in Somalia, an attempt at sovereign exclusion which ended disastrously for the Somalian state in general and the Barre regime in particular.
23. "Fire-and-forget is a type of missile guidance which does not require further guidance after launch such as illumination of the target or wire guidance, and can hit its target without the launcher being in line-of-sight of the target." Wikipedia. https://en.wikipedia.org/wiki/Fire-and-forget. Accessed January 30, 2019.
24. John R. Haines, 'How, Why and When Russia Will Deploy Little Green Men – and Why the US Cannot', *Foreign Policy Research Institute E-Note* (March 9, 2016), https://www.fpri.org/article/2016/03/how-why-and-when-russia-will-deploy-little-green-men-and-why-the-us-cannot/. Accessed January 21, 2019; see also Vitaly Shevchenko, "Little green men" or "Russian invaders"? *BBC*, March 11, 2014 https://www.bbc.com/news/world-europe-26532154, accessed January 22, 2019.
25. Stephen J. Blank. 'Imperial ambitions: Russia's Military Buildup', *World Affairs Institute* May/June 2015, pp. 67–75.
26. I use "forward policy" in the sense that Peter Hopkirk does when discussing the British attempts to safeguard their colonial possessions in India against Russian encroachment: "'British military planners'" argued that the only way to halt the Russian advance was by 'forward' policies. This meant getting there first, either by invasion, or by creating compliant 'buf-

fer' states, or satellites, astride the likely invasion routes." Peter Hopkirk, *The Great Game. On Secret Service in High Asia* (UK: Oxford University Press, 1990), p. 6.

27. Mikhail Klikushin, 'Little Green Men' From Russia Are Coming – And Lithuania Isn't Prepared', *The Observer* (04/21/17), https://observer.com/2017/04/russian-little-green-men-lithuania-invasion/. Accessed January 22, 2019.

28. Justin Huggler, 'Putin Privately Threatened to Invade Poland, Romania and the Baltic States', *Daily Telegraph*, 19 September 2014, http://www.telegraph.co.uk/news/worldnews/europe/russia/11106195/Putin-privately-threatened-to-invade-Poland-Romania-and-the-Balticstates.html. Accessed February 3, 2019.

29. Lawrence Freedman (2014) 'Ukraine and the Art of Limited War', *Survival: Global Politics and Strategy*, 56:6, 7–38.

30. Andrew Monaghan. Putin's Russia: shaping a 'grand strategy'? *International Affairs* 89: 5 (2013) 1221–1236.

31. Stephen J. Cimbala, 'Sun Tzu and Salami Tactics? Vladimir Putin and Military Persuasion in Ukraine', February 21–March 18, 2014, *The Journal of Slavic Military Studies*, 27:3, 359–379.

32. Dmitri Trenin. The Ukraine Crisis and the Resumption of Great Power Rivalry, Carnegie Institute (Moscow Center), 2014. http://carnegieendowment.org/files/ukraine_great_power_rivalry2014.pdf, accessed February 3, 2019.

33. David R. Cameron & Mitchell A. Orenstein (2012) 'Post-Soviet Authoritarianism: The Influence of Russia in Its "Near Abroad"', *Post-Soviet Affairs*, 28:1, 1–44.

34. Carol R. Saivetz. 'The ties that bind? Russia's evolving relations with its neighbors', *Communist and Post-Communist Studies* 45 (2012) 401–412.

35. Philip Shishkin. Central Asia's Crisis of Governance, Asia Society. January 2012. https://asiasociety.org/files/pdf/120215_central_asia_crisis_governance.pdf. Accessed February 3, 2019.

36. Jeffrey Gedmin. 'Beyond Crimea. What Vladimir Putin Really Wants'. *World Affairs*, July/August 2014, pp. 8–16.

37. Independent International Fact-Finding Mission on the Conflict in Georgia. September 2009. https://web.archive.org/web/20110706223037/http://www.ceiig.ch/pdf/IIFFMCG_Volume_II.pdf. Accessed January 22, 2019.

38. For an outline of the various dimensions and manifestations of Putinomania, see Robert A. Saunders, 'Is Vladimir Putin the super-villain we've all been waiting for?' http://www.e-ir.info/2015/09/22/vvp-is-vladimir-putin-the-super-villain-weve-all-been-waiting-for/. Accessed February 3, 2019.

39. Gedmin, 'Beyond Crimea'.

40. Alexander J. Motyl, 'Putin's zugzwang: The Russia-Ukraine Standoff', *World Affairs*, July/August 2014, pp. 58–65. *Zugzwang* is a German chess term denoting a condition in which one's king has to move, but cannot, because any move would result in check.
41. Kimberly Marten (2015) Putin's Choices: Explaining Russian Foreign Policy and Intervention in Ukraine, *The Washington Quarterly*, 38:2, 189–204.
42. Nina Khrushcheva. 'Inside Vladimir Putin's mind Looking Back in Anger' *World Affairs*, July/August 2014, pp. 17–24.
43. *The Economist*, "Putin's War on the West." https://www.economist.com/leaders/2015/02/12/putins-war-on-the-west. Accessed February 3, 2019.

CHAPTER 3

Interstice Exploiters

The previous chapter explored the creation of an interstitial front within the territory of a state by one of its rivals. In this chapter, I turn to states' responses to an already-existing interstice. In some cases, states encounter such interstices as third parties—for example, in the circumstance where an interstice was opened previously by two other parties (who may or may not still be engaged in their original war). In other cases, the interstice may lie between two different sovereign systems entirely, as was frequently the case when clusters of colonizing European states began to encountered indigenous African, Asian, and American sovereign systems from the fifteenth century onward. Lastly, interstice exploitation may represent the maturation of previous interstice-opening or interstice-closing actions by states, that is, that the states involved in interstitial warfare have changed not only what they seek within the interstice, but also the types of partnership which they engender to permit them access to it.

This latter point is crucial. One of the advantages that the interstitial war lens presented in this book enjoys over even the most faithful sub-typologizing conducted within the superficial or "chessboard" model discussed in Chap. 1 is its ability to go beyond unproductive (at best) or misleading (at worst) categories like "civil war with foreign involvement" and think about complex conflicts in finer terms relating to state agendas and how violence achieves them, even when these agendas change over time: that is, violent conflict as war*fare*, not just as one form of war or another. To do this, we once again rely on two key characteristics of

© The Author(s) 2020
D. Craig, *Sovereignty, War, and the Global State*,
https://doi.org/10.1007/978-3-030-19886-2_3

interstice exploiters which serve both as diagnostic indices to show that interstice exploitation is taking place, and as explications of just how the behaviors of interstitial actors serve to further the interstice-exploiting goals of their patrons. I refer to these two characteristics as interface sovereignty and capacity for compellence.

The first of these, interface sovereignty, is the interstice-exploiting analog of the "sovereign excludability" and "fungible sovereignty," exhibited by interstice openers and interstice closers and discussed in Chaps. 2 and 4, respectively. But whereas interstice openers must operate *outside* the regulatory frameworks of the sovereign system and interstice openers must operate *within* them, all that is required of interstice exploiters is to provide both concrete and institutional points of contact (i.e., interface) between the sovereign system and their own, whether these points take the form of wilderness forts at which payment can be exchanged for enemy scalps, the payment of stock dividends to reward state patrons for investment, or well-concealed airfields for connecting proxy forces with the arms shipments from their patron.

Providing such points of interface generally requires the interstice exploiter to produce and maintain institutions of rule of their own; but as long as these institutions can interface profitably with patron-state institutions on the "frontend," they may (as will be shown throughout this chapter) exhibit remarkable diversity of form on the "backend." Some interstice openers are little more than plunderers; others directly mimic the rule of their patron down to collecting taxes and making treaties. But regardless of how different the front-end institutions which define their conduct of war, establish their internal cohesion, and proclaim whichever authority under which they act, it is the inevitable presence of profit-conducting links between those institutions and a set of patrons outside the interstice which confirm the function of any given actor as exploitation.

The second key characteristic to be demonstrated in the cases gathered in this chapter is that of capacity for compellence. I draw the notion of compellence from Thomas Schelling's work on nuclear deterrence, in which he defined compellence as "the power to hurt" and advanced it as the mirror image of deterrence, which we might think of as the "power to retaliate."[1] Where deterrence threatens punishment to prevent an enemy from taking *future* action, compellence punishes an enemy for resisting a *current* action by the compeller, or continuing in a current action of its own, by making the choice to continue to resist (or to act) "painful" in terms of lost lives, property damage, and threat of escalation.

The reason that these two concepts merit separation, both in Schelling's model and in my use of it here, is that deterrence invites the enemy to select inaction because they have concluded that their means to violence is inferior to the deterring actor's—fewer missiles, a smaller army, and so on. Compellence, on the other hand, does not require the compeller's means to violence to be superior as long as it can be displayed that this violence can be exercised on the target with impunity and, by implication, the size of the target's defensive means are irrelevant. This is important because, as will be explored in the cases discussed here, interstitial actors are generally incapable of achieving *deterrence* because of the overwhelming advantage, militarily speaking, of states versus non-states during from the early Modern era onward. But when possessed of the right capabilities they can and do use compellence—not just on the various the unarmed inhabitants of the interstice, but also against any state forces that may attempt to confront them.

Specializing in compellence over deterrence has several implications for the institutions of interface sovereignty which serve as the core of the interstice-exploiting actor. Most importantly, when we consider (*a la* Weber) the role of the monopoly over authoritative violence in the constitution of formal states, we are in fact observing at least a notional commitment to internal deterrence: "do not cultivate the means to resist," the state warns, "or there will be violent consequences." But even when an interstice exploiter is ruling subjects like a state, its emphasis on compellence over deterrence means that it has no need of violent monopolies over those it compels; it has only to establish firmly in the minds of its opponents or challengers that resistance, even if successful, will be painful.

In what follows, I use five cases to demonstrate the interplay of interface sovereignty and capacity for compellence in interstice exploitation: the gun frontiers of Africa and North America (1650–1850), the Ottoman *ghazi* system (1400–1826), *petite guerre* in North America (1660–1814), the operations of the British East India Company in India (1700–1865), and the civil war in Mozambique (1975–1992).

GUN FRONTIERS

For readers in the postcolonial twenty-first century, it can be difficult to remember the tentative and widely dispersed manner in which European colonists first came to Africa, South and Southeast Asia, and North America. With names like "The Scramble for Africa" or "Manifest

Destiny," recountings of the collision between colonists and indigenous people imply not only a sense of pace in the colonial project but also the sense of an unstoppable forward momentum on the part of the colonizers; but it is significant that neither of these two periods take place until the nineteenth century, by which time Europeans had benefited from almost 400 years to prepare their positions in the colonial zone and erode the positions of those forces opposing them. During this first phase of colonial encroachment, Europeans cultivated or co-opted continent-spanning systems of interstitial warfare in order to provide themselves not only with desired commodities such as plunder and slaves, but also with a militarized frontier zone capable protecting them against rival colonial powers and the indigenous peoples who often outnumbered and outgunned them. It was only after centuries of softening up their indigenous enemies by means of this defensive interstitial warfare that colonial forces began to press forward into Africa and North America directly; by which time, whatever indigenous polities might have offered resistance were generally no longer in the militarily advantageous position that they had been in the seventeenth century.

Two striking examples of a defense in depth by means of interstice exploitation involve the seventeenth- and eighteenth-century exchanges between European powers, on one hand, and native political formations throughout the Eastern reaches of the North American continent or on the Guinea coast of West Africa, on the other. Along these two frontiers, rival European enclaves found themselves conducting what we might call "triadic rivalry," alternately allying with and opposing both one another and the indigenous states which opposed, hosted, or sought to ally with them in a complex set of occasionally violent three-way diplomacy.

The typical site around which these rivalries played out was either a series of small "factories" (i.e., trading posts) or fortified plantations, each belonging to a different European power but all built on or close to the coast and surrounded by one or more indigenous polities from which grants or leases had been extended by the ruler to the colonists. Exceptions to this model certainly existed. In some instances, colonial outposts nestled within each other, like the ill-fated English factory located within the Dutch settlement of Amboina; in others, they were located not on their own remote strip of coastal land but directly within the metropole of the host polity.

From these small enclaves the colonial traders would typically take in desired goods (e.g., spices or slaves) and exchange them for cargoes from Europe (e.g., tools, cloth, gold bullion, or firearms). It is the last commodity in each of these two sets of goods (i.e., slaves and firearms) that played the biggest role in the colonists waging of interstice-exploiting war, and it is also the pair that in many cases came to dominate all trade conducted across the frontier between colonists and indigenous peoples. Referring specifically to the trade between North American colonies and the Iroquois Confederation, David Silverman calls these firearm-for-slave trade networks "gun frontiers"[2]; in terms of the analysis conducted here, we can think of the gun frontier as the main bastion of the defense in depth system that constituted colonial interstice exploitation.

Gun frontiers recur with surprising regularity throughout the global colonial zone despite substantial variations between sites of conflict. Silverman's analysis, for example, concerns itself with the fraught and multipolar colonial interstice represented by the East coast of North America. Here, Dutch, French, English, and Spanish enclaves not only traded guns for slaves—the most simple activity of a gun frontier—but also used firearms as a form of capital investment (i.e., arming slave-taking indigenous peoples in order to expand their capacity to produce slaves), as a payment for security (i.e., arming friendly indigenous peoples who would nominally defend them from attack), and as a tool for exporting violence to rival colonial enclaves (i.e., arming indigenous peoples in the hope that these groups would attack these rival enclaves). In West Africa, on the other hand, it was rivalries between African polities that dominated the gun frontier, with colonial enclaves enjoying the freedom to play the field and extract increasingly profitable concessions from a succession of rivals who wished to gain their support.[3]

What is true of both gun frontiers, despite their different dynamics around multipolarity, are the ways in which it mattered that guns and slaves were the specific commodities in question. Most importantly in this regard, while the availability of guns, gunpowder, and the occasional cannon changed the capacity of indigenous interstitial actors to capture slaves and destroy any who opposed them, it both permitted and indeed required the development of new institutions of war and governance to make maximal use of the opportunity represented by the slave trade. Some indigenous polities (such as the Bakongo or Zulu people of Southern Africa) who gained access to guns adopted them into existing coercive practice without substantially changing how they fought or ruled, but for others the attractiveness of adding firearm warfare as a state capacity resulted in a complete redesign of their societies along <u>interface sovereignty</u> lines in order to smooth the transfer of slaves and guns back and forth between their clients and themselves. The result was an entirely different polity to what had existed before; by 1850, for example, the King of Dahomey could tell a foreign visitor that "[my] people are a military people ... and the slave trade feeds them." Dahomey had started its political existence as a minor tributary to the cavalry-ruled Oyo Empire, but by the closing of the gun frontier, it had become a predator polity of unrivaled strength, entirely devoted to a simple political logic: use guns to acquire slaves through victorious war, and then sell the slaves to acquire more guns. On the North American gun frontier, this same process played out with the Iroquois, whose gunmen turned slave-taking into a core Iroquois occupation and who began to essentially cleanse the eastern seaboard of smaller tribes in order to sustain their gun-for-slave trade with the English colonies in particular.

With slaves taken in this fashion representing the human capital of whichever group or polity they were being seized from, this meant that by trading guns for slaves, the tiny colonial outposts had produced a self-propagating wave of polity-eroding weakness which turned every group that it touched into either slave-taker or a victim of slave-taking. Although the predators were able to benefit from this system for longer than their victims, inflation[4] left local markets vulnerable to global events that either provided new competitors (as occurred in the eighteenth century, when slaves from Africa began to flood the American markets) or shut them down the trade entirely (as occurred with the abolition of Transatlantic slavery by Britain). With no key industries left within the state except slaving, and no buyers for what slaves could still be found, the predators had no options but to collapse and be picked off by their clients.

Cultural factors inarguably played a role in this destructive asynchronicity between the technologies for violence and the technologies of rule. For one thing, some combination of factors independent of the colonists and their guns must be able to explain why some interstitial actors sought to become firearm-empowered revisionist powers within their own sovereign system and others did not. However, if one can be satisfied with answering the simpler question of "how" rather than the more complex one of "why," one clear reason for this disconnect is to be found in the difference between compellence and deterrence.

The creation of stable systems of rule—even complex tributary systems like the overlapping "fields of empire" which characterized West Africa at the time[5]—requires not only deterrence but also the predictability which deterrence builds into the contract between ruler and potential internal rival. It is the fear of individual consequences—even if a general revolt by a coalition of rivals were to succeed—which convinces individual rivals to stay home and even to defend the *status quo*. But calculating consequences requires a fine sense of who would have the upper hand in any violent contest, and by pouring an unfamiliar military technology into the interstice between their enclaves and the sovereign systems of the territories they were colonizing; the colonists were making such calculations essentially impossible. The same uncertainty does not apply to the would-be revisionist or the slave-taking band, as multiple incidents in human history show; for such groups, the inability of their victims to assess how dangerous can be a critical advantage.

Thus, the "beneficiaries" of the gun-for-slave trade gained the short-term <u>capacity for compellence</u>, but not the long-term capacity to deter either their subjects and rivals, or in turn the European traders themselves; this gain was not only key to the manner in which they functioned within the interstice, but also to the eventual ascendance of the Europeans as undisputable masters of the territories in which they had once been mere guests.

THE GHAZIS

While the gun frontiers show interstice exploitation as a self-accelerating and therefore eventually unsustainable practice, this is not the practice's only possible configuration. Indeed, interstice exploitation can also be maintained more or less stably across the long term. At roughly the same time as the first European colonists were beginning to trade guns for slaves in Africa and North America, for example, the continent-spanning Ottoman Empire had been using interstitial actors to provide a stable belt of border protection for several centuries and would go on to use these forces for several centuries more. These interstitial actors were the *ghazis*, who started off as broadly indistinguishable from other groups within the heterogeneous proto-Turkish nomad polities, but who would eventually constitute the weaponized outermost shell of an integrated continuum of interstitial actors (*ghazis, bashi-bazouks*, Janissaries, and corsairs) integral to the frontier policy of the mature Ottoman Empire.

A useful concept for discussing how actors with one (or both) feet outside the state might nonetheless serve as a defense for it is Edward Luttwak's notion of "defence in depth."[6] Luttwak coined this term as a part of his analyses of the border security regimes of the late Roman Empire to the refer to the notion that imperial forces would fall back from the empire's frontiers when attacked and use pre-prepared areas of engagement within Roman territory to reduce and eventually defeat their attackers instead of attempting to hold them on the border.

Modern archeological reassessments of Luttwak's argument have cast substantial doubts on whether such a policy ever actually existed. In addition, the interstitial strategy described in this chapter does not meet Luttwak's exact criteria because the legions in his model were, after all, the formal forces of the state conducting warfare with the state's own territory. One might say that relying on groups outside the state for defense more closely resembles Luttwak's depiction of Rome's earlier "forward defense" policy—except that in the Roman case these external security partners were client kingdoms in their own right and not interstitial non-states. However, by adding "interstitial" to Luttwak's concept—hence, "interstitial defense in depth"—I hope to bridge these two models to give the sense of <u>an area outside the state and its sovereign system (i.e., the interstice) made ready for warfare and maintained in this configuration as long as its defensive capacities are needed by that state.</u> This defensive interstice is able to combine the militarization of interstitial actors seen in the colonial gun frontiers with resilience over time, because the actors responsible for its operation are integrated with the state from the very start; thus, in terms of my model, because their <u>interface sovereignty</u> has been built to last as opposed to simply being built to generate slave flows.

A brief history of the individual actors which constituted the Ottoman interstitial defense in depth system is useful in illustrating what I mean by "built to last." Douglas Streusand's comparative examination of "Islamic Gunpowder Empires" places the origin of the *ghazi* as a religiously observant frontier raider within the Mamluk kingdoms of Egypt. In this context, initially slight distinctions between "the concepts of *jihad* (literally, "striving," with the expression *fisabillilah*, meaning "in the path of God," implied) and *ghaza* (raiding)" would in time become significant, given that:

> A policy of jihad generally implied a vigorous commitment to <u>government</u> in accord with Shariah … [in contrast,] Ghaza, though itself an Arabic word, generally referred to frontier raiding, whether as a highly organized government activity (e.g., the Ghaznavid and Ghurid raids from the Afghan hinterlands into the Ingo-Gangetic plain) or as the activity of autonomous frontier raiders (e.g., on the Anatolian frontier).[7]

While raider polities like the proto-Ottomans were initially able to ignore these terminological and theological niceties, their slow transition

from roving to static banditry[8] under their first leader, Osman Bey, eventually forced an about-turn as the Osmanli ("followers of Osman") went
from being frontier bands at the edge of Mamluk territory to being power
holders in their own Anatolian polity around the thirteenth and fourteenth centuries. Thus, while Osman had ruled from horseback as a war
leader, his son Orkhan minted coinage and commissioned commemorative liturgy following the conquest of the city of Bursa in 1327. Another
key inflection point in this development of a central state distinct from
raiding appears to have been the civil war for control of the Ottoman polity between Sultan Murad II and Musa Bey in the early fifteenth century.
Although both factions fielded irregular forces, the outcome of this war
favored Murad's centralized taxation-gathering state forces against Musa's
frontier raiders; going forward, it would be the Ottoman metropole which
dictated terms to the Anatolian raiders and not the other way around.

But what were these terms? In terms of governance, the *ghazis* had
both a negative and a positive use; in other words, the *ghazis'* willingness
to accept a form of exile to the periphery of the state served the Ottoman
state both through their absence from the core, and through the actual
actions they took in the periphery.

The *ghazis'* negative role was ideological: by accepting a subordinate
role to the Sultan and his military and confining their predations to non-
Ottoman targets, the *ghazis* permitted the empire to both fulfill both its
ostensible role as a violent defender of Islam on and beyond its frontiers,
and its role as a cosmopolitan and multi-faith guarantor of its subjects'
liberties within those same frontiers. Thus, of the frontier ghazis, a contemporary author could write:

> Who is a Ghāzī? ... [A] Ghāzī is the instrument of the religion of Allah, a
> servant of God who purifies the earth from the filth of polytheism ... the
> Ghāzī is the sword of God, He is the protector and the refuge of the believ-
> ers. If he becomes a martyr in the ways of God, do not believe that he has
> died—he lives in beatitude with Allah, he has eternal life.[9]

At the same time as the ghazis were "purifying the earth" of the interstice, in the areas behind their holdings where the Ottoman state ruled
directly, the policy of *mudarra* ("friendship") could be the law of the land,
representing "security, reasonable and predictable taxation, and the right
to petition for relief from abuses" for Muslims, Christians, and Jews alike.[10]
The result was an empire in which economic and political liberties could
coexist with an ideological bastion that stretched from Orkhan (who

designated himself "Sultan, son of the Sultan of the Ghāzīs, Ghāzī, son of Ghāzī, maquis of the horizons, hero of the world")[11] right up to Mustafa Kemal Ataturk (who was granted the title "Ghāzī" by the Turkish Grand National Assembly in 1921).

While the *ghazis*' absence from the core of the state served this negative role, their presence in the hinterlands was serving a positive role by providing defense not specifically against the armies of neighboring states but against raider confederations who were in many ways mirror images of the ghazis themselves, that is, the *akritoi* of the empire's western borders or the Cossacks of its northern borders, who were to the Byzantine Empire and Muscovy exactly what the *ghazis* were to the Ottomans.

As groups well-adapted to interstitial life and warfare, it is little surprise that the *ghazis*, *akritoi*, Cossacks, and Tartars often bore more resemblance to one another than to their state sponsors. All were compellence-dependent raiders rather than deterrence-dependent governors by nature; all funneled a portion of their plunder back to their patrons as a mix of tribute and payment for luxuries and finished goods. Furthermore, all served as hotbeds of cultural and religious heterodoxy, outlaws who sought on the interstitial frontier those forms of liberty which would have made them enemies of the centralized state had they instead tried to remain within it.[12] Even the quasi-sovereign jurisdictions administered by these interstitial actors on behalf of their patrons resembled one another more than they resembled those of the imperial core, such that when the Ottomans conquered Byzantine territory they were able to simply reallocate the fiefdom units assigned to individual *akritoi* (referred to as *pronoia*) to the *ghazi* as *timar* land grants on a one-for-one basis.[13]

These similarities between the ghazis and their opposite numbers are particularly interesting when considering the eventual triumph of *ghazis* over the *akritoi* in their thirteenth- and fourteenth-century heyday. During these periods of Ottoman expansion, the front lines at which Byzantine power gave way to Ottoman were interstitial ones, driven as much by wide-scale *akritoi* defections to the enemy as by decisive clashes between imperial armies. The defections, originating in part from factional power struggles within Byzantine Empire which divided the loyalty of the *akritoi* and thereby eroded the basis of their interface sovereignty with the Byzantine state, also revealed the ghazi capacity for compellence in ideological as well as physical terms. With the *akritoi* finding themselves a step closer to being able to integrate into the forces of their *ghazi* opponents than into the highly specialized regular troops from Constantinople, why persist in enduring the pain of *ghazi* raids when one could simply step aside—or even, through conversion, join the winning side and share in the plunder?

The *ghazis* displayed this ability to compel defection and alliance throughout their area of operations. Expanding into coastal areas of Lydia and Pamphylia in the late thirteenth century, they had allied with local seafarers and demobilized Byzantine veterans to form small pirate fleets, founded the pirate state of Menteshe by allying with migrant Turks from the interior, and contested control of Rhodes with the Knights of St John. The Mentesheans went on to contribute both a regular and a pirate fleet for later incorporation into the Ottoman navies; another pirate-kingdom was produced from an "alliance of land- and sea-Ghāzīs" in the emirate of Aydın, which required the "alliance of Venice, Cyprus and the Knights of St. John, at papal instigation, to put a stop to their efforts."[14]

Having limned the ghazis' utility to the Ottoman state in both a negative (ideology-sustaining) and positive (border-expanding) sense, the fuller dimensions of the "integrated continuum of interstitial actors (*ghazis, bashi-bazouks*, Janissaries, and corsairs)" mentioned previously are now apparent. For the *ghazis* were not the only actors to provide these two sorts of utility to the state. Like the ghazis, the *bashi-bazouks* were irregular soldiers in the empire's armies, often paid in plunder or tax exemption and thus serving as an informal arm of the state; the Janissary corps, somewhat more formally, were a militarized slave class drawn from the empire's Christian subjects; and the corsairs were sea captains like the Mentesheans, who made their living as privateers and adventurers on what Crowley calls the "fragmenting maritime frontier between Islam and Christendom" of the sixteenth century.[15] All of these actors enhanced the capabilities of the state precisely because they were in part outside it, that is, able to exercise their capacities for compellence on the empire's enemies while bound to it by carefully maintained institutions of integrative sovereignty. Furthermore, it is no exaggeration to say that these actors not only sprang from the Ottoman Empire's creation of interstices, but through the exercise of their particular skills at interstitial warfare, ensured that the empire could seek new interstitial lands and convert the old ones to productive sources of goods and taxes.

The Janissaries, for example, had their origin in the loose and interstitial rule extended over captured Christian territories by the Ottomans, by which the inhabitants of these territories paid a manpower tax in sons who were then carefully groomed as a caste of elite slave warriors whose loyalty to the Sultan was unquestionable: it was, after all, the Janissaries that prevented Musa Bey from unseating Sultan Murad II at the critical moment when the central state began to eclipse the empire's *ghazi* forebears, thereby ensuring the conversion of the Ottoman heartland into a stable imperial core. Similarly, while famous corsair families like the brothers Oruch and Hizir (later Hayrettin) Barbarossa began their experience of the Ottoman Empire's interstitial wars as galley slaves aboard Christian raiders in the Aegean, by the time of their retirement they would be serving the empire by managing corsair fleets and coastal strongholds as far away as Algiers—not only an impressive arc for the sons of a Greek cavalryman from Lesbos, but also a stark illustration of just how far the empire's interstitial defense-in-depth system had been extended during their lifetime.[16]

To summarize, then, in thinking about the role of interstice exploitation for defensive purposes, we see that what set the *ghazi* system apart from the gun frontiers of the colonial zone and the *akritoi* networks was its resilience, a resilience derived not from variances in capacity for compellence, but rather by variances in the nature of the interface sovereignty connecting each actor back to its patron state. On the gun frontier, this interface was crude and entirely driven by the search for short term profit; for the *akritoi*, it could only be as strong as the fragmenting legitimacy of the state behind it; for the *ghazis* the interface was multiply reinforced by religio-ideological and patrimonial recognition from the center, and was hence able to reliably serve the state for centuries.

The *ghazis'* long period of service notwithstanding, the generalizability of their experience to interstitial warfare conducted by polities with a different cultural and religious background may well prompt the question: can one have a stable system of interstitial defense-in-depth without the many contingent factors (such as nomadism and Islam) which shaped the Ottoman Empire's relationship with its frontier forces? To answer this question, we return to the North American colonial zone, and to the seventeenth- and eighteenth-century French doctrine of *petite guerre*.

PETITE GUERRE

While the Thirty Years' War in Europe (1618–1648) is most remembered for the formal geopolitical delineations of the post-Westphalian order that it created, it was also a period of intense strategic and military innovation during which European powers experimented with interstitial warfare.

Indeed, as the discussion of the figure of the "partisan" conducted in Chap. 4 will illustrate, the war's continent-wide fronts between poorly demarcated factions gave combatant powers multiple opportunities to deploy large regular armies both against and alongside various kinds of informally constituted irregular troops like partisans. By the eighteenth century, these lessons of the Thirty Years' War had moved from the regional fronts in which individual lessons were learned and individual kinds of interstitial actor encountered, into the continent-wide doctrinal mainstream. Thus, for example, the Hungarian term *pandur*, meaning a Balkan frontier guard serving in the Habsburg armies as an irregular fighter, could also appear as the name of a French naval vessel (*Pandour*) in 1780 and the name of a Dutch militia corps (*het Corps Pandoeren*) at the Cape of Good Hope in 1793.[17]

While many countries recognized the utility of mixing regular and irregular forces, it was French military theorists who coined the term *petite guerre* ("small war") to refer to the ways in which these irregular forces should best be employed, and to distinguish this theory of war from similar theories about the employment of regular forces. For these theorists, *petite guerre* always existed in a subsidiary or supporting role to the main event of clashing regular forces, constituting "all the movements that merely back up the operations of an army" and nothing more.[18]

This definition, however, was predicated on the actual existence of an army for the *petite guerre* to support; and in the French colonial territories of North America at this time, no such army was to be found. It was in these colonial territories that *petite guerre*, transplanted to the sovereign interstices between the French and English areas of direct control, would develop from a sideshow to a grand strategy in its own right: a doctrine of interstitial defense in depth, founded on the same key characteristics of interface sovereignty and capacity for compellence that we have observed in the interstices of the gun frontiers and the *ghazi* system.

The key factor in explaining this renaissance of the practice of *petite guerre* in the Americas was cost. Despite the wealth and relative power of the French state throughout the seventeenth and eighteenth centuries, its military budget was dominated by Continental concerns rather than colonial ones, and its expansions into colonial markets were often conducted by private citizens operating under royal charters, rather than by the formal forces of the state. The French treasury was also highly loss-averse, with reverses in fortune in Europe translating to an immediate contraction of commitments in the colonial zone throughout this period. In both the

Caribbean and the North American frontier, this left French administrators desperately on the lookout for ways to conduct war, or at the very least to defend their territory, on the cheap.[19] The maritime solution was interstice-opening warfare, conducted via a flotilla of privateers and financed by a specialized merchant class called *armateurs* who banded together to finance individual warships[20]; on land, the solution was interstice exploitation conducted not by French troops at all but by indigenous intermediaries weaponized through the payment of bounties for dead enemies of the state—an interstitial defense-in-depth.

Putting such a system into place was, however, more complex than simply giving the order to French militia commanders to start arming and directing willing indigenous partners. For one thing, while interstitial defense-in-depth did begin by taking the basic model of *petite guerre* contained in Continental military doctrine and eventually formalized in texts such as the 1752 *Traite de la Petite Guerre* by La Croix and the 1756 *Treatise on the Military Service of Light Horse and Light Infantry* by de Grandmaison, it also required upending the specific prohibitions contained in such texts against allowing irregular forces to plunder, rape, or execute prisoners.[21] These prohibitions, derived from the same growing corpus of Enlightenment thought that was restructuring political philosophy at this time, made a great deal of sense in a European theater where the need to peacefully rule subjugated populations was of interest to military planners. But for the purposes of interstitial defense-in-depth, such prohibitions merely tied the hands of interstitial fighters who counted on cruelty as a force multiplier and on plunder as a means of holding warbands together—or, to restate this in terms of my model, who counted on cruel modes of warfare to provide <u>capacity for compellence</u> and whose <u>interface sovereignty</u> cohered around the taking of slaves and the provision of bounties for enemy scalps by French administrators. Accordingly, while many French leaders within the colonies publicly expressed repulsion and dismay at various acts of "savagery" enacted on France's enemies by its indigenous allies, others not only permitted such acts but also encouraged and participated in them. The result was a system of violence—not just *petite guerre* but *la guerre sauvage* ("savage war") which French commanders found not only effective and resilient, but at times *too* resilient.

The French experience of working with indigenous allies in the North American theater of the Seven Years' War (1754–1763) provides an excellent example of this problematic resilience, especially because this was a rare occasion in which French military planners actually had access to exactly the kinds of regular forces that *petite guerre* had been designed to complement. However, all attempts to change the operating model of their indigenous auxiliaries to a less predatory format either failed or backfired. Dismayed by torture and hostage-taking after the French victory at Fort Oswego in 1756, for example, the French commander had paid a ransom to secure the freedom of British prisoners after the battle. Word of this decision spread, and by spring, over 2000 indigenous fighters from 33 separate nations had mustered in Montreal to join the French forces. This, as it turned out, was not only a force too large to turn down, but also too large to keep in check. After British forces surrendered at Fort William Henry the following year, more than 500 prisoners were seized by indigenous forces while leaving the fort under French escort, and either killed on the spot or ransomed back to the French in the days and weeks that followed.[22]

The disaster at Fort William Henry spelled the beginning of the end for the French system of interstitial defense-in-depth. For one thing, a small-pox outbreak within the fort soon spread throughout the indigenous peoples of the Great Lakes via the fighter contingents they had contributed to the siege; there would be no repeats of the record-breaking 1756 muster at Montreal. For another, the poor conduct of the indigenous fighters had finally provoked a irreconcilable split between the ascendant factions of the French military in Canada who favored regular war (such as the Maquis de Montcalm) and those who favored irregular war (such as the Maquis de Vandreuil). Going forward, the war would be fought (and lost, by France) in the conventional European manner.

The lessons learned through a century of unrestrained *petite guerre* in the North American interstice would in time reappear as mainstream military doctrine on both sides of the war—to the extent that, for example, an officer commanding troops equipped and trained according to the new "bush fighting" doctrines promoted by British Brigadier General Howe would complain in 1758 that his troops could not be distinguished from "common plough men."[23] But *petite guerre* as a cornerstone of interstate warfare between colonial enclaves could not, in the end, survive the increasingly consolidated nature of the colonial presence on the continent and the higher incentives this brought to formalize war between Europeans and render it more in line with continental norms of honor, good conduct, and Enlightenment sovereignty.[24]

Regardless of this eventual decline, though, it was inarguably the exploitation of the North American interstice for the purpose of interstitial defense-in-depth which carried the European colonies through the seventeenth and eighteenth centuries and which permitted, as with the gun frontiers, the eventual expansion of direct colonial rule into the territories of exhausted indigenous opponents in the nineteenth century. More importantly, for the purposes of the argument conducted here, the military partnerships between the French administrators and Native American forces provides a defense of the idea that the ghazi experience discussed previously is indeed generalizable without the specific contingencies of religion and nomadic raiding.

One further case requires discussion, however, before the generalizability advanced in this chapter can be considered complete. Thus far, all the only interstice-exploiting projects surveyed have been defensive in nature, that is, built to permit an interstice-exploiting state to defend itself, via a form of defense-in-depth, against threats for which the use of its regular forces would not be suitable. What would an aggressive rather than defensive interstice-exploiting project look like? For this, I now briefly turn to the British East India Company (BEIC) and its profit-seeking campaigns in India from 1700, before concluding this chapter with the contemporary case of Mozambique.

The Honorable Company

Given the astonishing heights of military and economic power that it would one day reach, it is important to not lose sight of what a failure the EIC might have been had circumstances been otherwise. For example, even though it may seem to lie somewhat outside the focus of this section, which is the Company's career as a tool of interstice exploitation rather its existence more generally, the fact that in 1657 the Company made moves to declare bankruptcy and had to be saved by a redesign of its Charter shows that the EIC's simple existence as a private-public partnership oriented toward the eastern spice trade was not what made it profitable or powerful. Nor was the BEIC a trail-blazing innovation on the world stage whose rise to power was based on being the first such partnership to connect the Indonesian Spice Islands to a European trading metropole. In fact, at this low point in the Company's fortunes, other chartered companies like the Dutch *Vereenigte Oost-Indische Compagnie* (VOC) not only had longer careers and more lucrative ones, having themselves wrested the spice trade from earlier Portuguese control while the comparatively tiny English merchant presence slipped into only those harbors from which the Dutch and Portuguese had not yet barred them.[25]

Instead, what drove the EIC to eventually eclipse not only the VOC but all other such entities and become a *de facto* sovereign power with a larger army and deeper coffers than many states, was the unique way in which it was able to leverage not just its position as partly of and partly outside the state, but the specific capacities for compellence and forms of interface sovereignty that it used to exploit sovereign interstices through violent means.

The EIC's first step toward primacy in the world of chartered companies required a mandate for the acquisition of state-like levels of armament. This was granted in the redesigned charter that saved the company in 1657, in which it gained legal authority to settle and fortify its positions in the East Indies as it saw fit. The fact that its previous charter had not granted the EIC such powers may seem odd, given that the VOC had exactly this ability from the outset and had already used it to great effect to lock the EIC out of several profitable areas; but in this regard one must also recall that during the English Civil War that had just ended, charter company colonies like Bermuda had rebelled against the English state and had to be blockaded using privateers and then reconquered by Parliamentary naval forces in 1651.

Acquiring these arms, however, was not enough on its own. Even under its new charter, the EIC failed to make substantial headway against its French, Dutch, and Portuguese rivals between 1657 and 1700. The problems it faced were twofold. First, while its new charter had allowed the EIC to gain military parity with its rivals, none of the chartered companies had the power to exterminate another, although raids and sea battles aplenty ensured a high turnover among the companies and even some dynamism in terms of their distribution around the East Indies. Second, none of the companies' ventures were so profitable as to make their eventual primacy over the others a *fait accompli*. Even the VOC, whose administrator in the East Indies, Jan Pieterzon Coen, was as much a military strategist as a merchant, was not able to make enough money from its operations to sustain the cost and scope of maintaining the iron grip over the region to which Coen believed the Dutch Republic was legally entitled. Consequently, although Coen achieved all his goals and brought the VOC enormous status and wealth, the company still collapsed under 12 million guilders of debt at the end of the eighteenth century.[26]

Instead, the key to the EIC's rise relative to its rivals lay outside itself. By early eighteenth century, the Mughal Empire which had dominated the Indian subcontinent was in decline, and the EIC found itself in an unexpectedly advantageous position to take advantage of this. Based out of Madras after being pushed out of the lucrative Indonesian spice trade by the larger and more aggressive VOC, EIC operations at this time focused on a barely profitable exchange of heavy English cloth for trade goods throughout the Red Sea and to a few Mughal ports, as well as on servicing a royal contract for the Indian saltpeter that the English state needed for its gunpowder mills. The EIC's largest rival in this marginal region of the East Indies was the French *Compagnie des Indes Orientales* (CIO), which had fortified several areas around Pondicherry.

Periods of relative violence and peace between the two companies alternated until, in 1748, the CIO forced the EIC's hand, by attempting to install pro-French rulers on the princedoms within which Madras and Pondicherry lay. Control of these thrones would have allowed them to revoke the sovereign decrees upon the EIC's local operations depended. The EIC retaliated by sponsoring its own candidate for the throne—Muhammad Ali. But the EIC did more than sponsor Muhammad Ali; it also contributed 200 of the company's private militia and 300 locally hired mercenaries under the command of Robert Clive, an EIC clerk-turned-captain who had seen action in the region during battles between the EIC and CIO two years earlier. After a grueling forced march, Clive's troops took the fort at Arcot—the capital city of Muhammad Ali's largest rival—and then weathered a three months of siege before reinforcements arrived from the EIC and from Muhammad Ali's allies. Following a series of running battles over the next few months, the French plan was thwarted and the grateful Muhammad Ali gained imperial recognition of his right to rule. Amidst the opportunities presented by the fragmentation of the Mughal Empire, Robert Clive had discovered the EIC's true comparative advantage over its rivals: king-making.

For the next 17 years, the EIC turned the picking of sides in squabbles between competing princes into a highly profitable business model. Opposed at each turn by the CIO, but driven forward by Clive's enormous ambitions and apparent genius for quickly responding to opportunities for advancing his position as quickly they came up, the EIC was able in 1765 to drive a wedge between the Mughal emperor himself, Shah Alam, and a member of his ruling council, Mir Jafar. The subsequent battle of Plassey left the emperor and his French allies defeated, and the EIC and its allies as the lords of Bengal. In return for his services to Mir Jafar, Clive was personally granted a *jagir*, or land grant, worth an annual £27 000; from the EIC's point of view, following a "victory that owed more to treachery, forged contracts, bankers and bribes than military prowess, [Clive] transferred to the EIC treasury no less than £2.5 m seized from the defeated rulers of Bengal—in today's currency, around £23 m for Clive and £250 m for the company."[27]

The reign and fall of the EIC and of Robert Clive go beyond the scope of this book, suffice it to say that like the VOC, the EIC's path to ruin lay through bankruptcy and subsequent absorption by its parent state. The EIC applied for its first bailout in the face of rising costs and declining profits in 1772; the subsequent Parliamentary inquiry ruined Clive both financially and emotionally, and he committed suicide in his home in 1774. Following the Indian Mutiny of 1865, all the lands painstakingly conquered by the EIC's colossal ground forces—260,000 strong at their height—had reverted to the British crown, consigning the EIC to the history books. What is of more relevance to the argument of this book is not that the EIC eventually failed, but in determining how it succeeded as dramatically as it did without the aggressive military orientation and focus on direct rule exhibited by the VOC. The answer to this question lies in the EIC's capacity for compellence and the nature of its interface sovereignty.

Regarding compellence, it is important to not forget that Indian armies were not the under-equipped indigenous forces of Africa or the Americas; they had cannon, firearms, cavalry, and all the advantages enjoyed by their European opponents. Understanding how the EIC managed to compel obedience, then, requires attention not just to the technologies employed by the company on the battlefield but the genius of its leaders—primarily Clive—in picking the right battlefields to be on and the right faction to be on them with. What Clive's forces threatened, in their engagement with Indian potentates, was not so much physical pain or the death of soldiers but coup de main via treachery, surprise attack, and alliance. Clive's first military victory, at Arcot, only happened because the fort's garrison had been frightened off by rumors that his force was much larger than it really was; his largest victory, at Plassey, was guaranteed by the defection of Mir Jafar's troops from the imperial line literally during the battle. For the EIC's opponents, a fair fight was not what one had to fear, but an unfair one: the EIC derived its capacity for compellence from their flexibility, from their ability to betray, and most importantly from their ability to support and amplify betrayal amidst the growing sovereign interstices opened up by the failing Mughal Empire.

Turning to interface sovereignty, we once again see the strength of the EIC in terms of flexibility. The open-ended 1657 charter had given it the power to conduct war, indeed, but also a more important power: to sign treaties. It was this *de jure* weapon in the sovereign arsenal that Clive and his successors would use to incredible effect. At the same time, the company had the commercial muscle to turn plunder taken in India—it is no accident that the word *loot* appeared in English as a Hindi loanword at around this time—into dividends in London and then, via the enormous overlap between the moneyed classes and the politically influential classes in Britain—turn those dividends right back into a mandate for violent plunder. The EIC's company troops enjoyed a parallel structure to the British army throughout this time, with individual officers transferring back and forth in pursuit of battlefield experience or simple financial advancement, and although sneering at the Company as mere tradesmen remained the social order of the day for Britain's domestic and colonial elites well into the nineteenth century,[28] the line of those willing to take advantage of the Company's legacy maintained its superior length relative to the line of those seeking to condemn it for as long as the markets of India continued to be profitable.

It is no exaggeration to say that without the EIC, it is unlikely that India would have ever become the sole possession of Britain; and without India's struggle to throw off British rule, it is also no exaggeration to say that the anticolonial conflicts in Africa and Asia would have looked very different to how they did. As the final case to be addressed in this chapter, I now turn to one such struggle to examine how interstices can be exploited not for defense-in-depth security or profit via plunder, but for foreign policy signaling and the maintenance of regional hegemony.

RENAMO

The abrupt withdrawal of government forces from Portugal's colonies in 1975 following a leftist coup in Lisbon, left both Angola and Mozambique in an uncertain position regarding who, precisely, would succeed the colonists in running the country. This split was more apparent in Angola, where the Union for the Total Independence of Angola (UNITA) and the Popular Movement for the Liberation of Angola (MPLA) had been fighting one another as well as the Portuguese for more than ten years. In Mozambique, however, the split was less apparent. Nominally, the country only had one group that had resisted the Portuguese: the Mozambique Liberation Front, or FRELIMO, which duly assumed control of the newly independent Mozambican state.

Underneath this apparent unity, however, lay two dangerous fault lines. The first was between the FRELIMO state and the various indigenous military units such as the *flechas* ("Arrows") who had fought alongside the Portuguese troops and feared for their future under FRELIMO rule; the second was between FRELIMO and the many ex-FRELIMO soldiers and supporters who had been alienated from the party through its post-independence programs of nationalization and communalization. Finnegan characterizes this process of alienation as follows:

> After independence, Frelimo approached the rural administration with what has been called "the ideology of the tabula rasa." Traditional society was "feudal." Religion was obscurantismo. Chiefs and *curandeiros* [traditional healers] were shunted aside .... [at a conference in Botswana in 1987, the leader of the Frelimo delegation declared] "The traditional chiefs do not have any role to play in [Mozambique]... we are not concerned with our traditional chiefs, but with the interests of the people."[29]

Such expressions of distaste for "traditional" ways of existence in Mozambique earned FRELIMO many enemies, both within their own party and without. Into this growing interstice stepped the covert security forces of neighboring Rhodesia, whose white minority government was searching for a Mozambican proxy to pursue their own enemies—the Zimbabwe African National Union (ZANU), which used Mozambican territory as a safe haven against Rhodesian counterattack. Rhodesian Special Forces trainers gathered and armed disaffected Mozambicans in specially constructed training camps before sending them back in to their own country to fight against both FRELIMO and ZANU's armed wing, the Zimbabwe African National Liberation Army (ZANLA). This group became known as the Movement of National Resistance, or RENAMO.

RENAMO and its Rhodesian handlers found no shortage of grievances to capitalize on within their area of operations. By 1977, the year *before* RENAMO began large-scale military operations across Mozambique, FRELIMO party rhetoric was already highlighting a shift from fighting the colonial oppressor to fighting *O Inimigo Interno* ("the enemy within"), which was defined as "those class enemies of Frelimo's revolution who were working through rumour, conspiracy, and economic sabotage to undermine it."[30] Those who resisted the government's programs were often placed in detention camps; those who did not fit into the schemes were often the target of arbitrary social engineering efforts such as the 1983 'Operation Production' in which 50,000 unemployed city dwellers were transported out into the countryside and "told to start farming."[31]

Despite the over-zealousness of these approaches to the post-independence order, some analysts have queried the degree to which they truly caused animosities and rifts within Mozambican society; Allport, for instance, characterizes such views of the decline in FRELIMO's popularity as being overly "traditionalist."[32] Nonetheless, such grievances—whether they would have led to the growth of a RENAMO-style organization in time or not—played right into the Rhodesians' hands; by using traditional Ndau networks to recruit those opposed to the Machel government, and by directing their growing anti-FRELIMO force to liberate detention camps where more like-minded recruits could be found, the CIO provided a touchstone and rallying point for anti-FRELIMO sentiment.[33]

By 1978, then, RENAMO groups were operating throughout most of the country, capitalizing on their Rhodesian support and training and the FRELIMO government's relatively weak control over the rural areas. Their primary aim was a simple one: distraction and destabilization. In the words of one of Rhodesian special forces trainer, "Our aim was simple ... we wanted them to keep Machel and Frelimo so busy they couldn't devote time or attention to supporting Zanla."[34] This continued to be RENAMO's function long after the Rhodesian state which created it had passed out of existence; rather than fade away after the advent of majority rule in Rhodesia, the RENAMO cadres and many of their handlers were quickly adopted into the South African security apparatus.

The South African Defence Force (SADF) hoped to use RENAMO much as the Rhodesians had: a cost-effective and essentially deniable proxy combatant with which to bedevil the Machel regime—and, given Zimbabwe's reliance on Mozambique for sea-borne trade, the Mugabe regime as well. In a 1983 interview, one RENAMO defector told his interviewer of a meeting with an SADF colonel who claimed that "Pretoria had no wish to change the government of Mozambique, but simply to 'put Machel on his knees.'"[35]

In keeping with these mission parameters, handed down to RENAMO first by the Rhodesians and then by the South Africans, most of the organization's targets were economic and civilian sites, and its operations were more designed to make the country ungovernable than necessarily to unseat the government. Such goals were not entirely incompatible with RENAMO's own. Having not existed in any coherent form before the intervention of the Rhodesians; RENAMO's "ideology," such as it was, was defined almost entirely in opposition to FRELIMO's zealous Marxist-Leninism, and for this reason RENAMO leaders seemed more than willing to simply strive, though a process of attrition, to attain a position of military strength from which it could dictate terms to the incumbent FRELIMO government regarding the various policies to which it was opposed. While it was fundamentally a military organization, therefore, by virtue of the circumstances of its creation its aims were (and remained) strictly political.[36]

If a simmering hinterland war against soft targets can be said to have suited FRELIMO's opponents, it can also be said to have—perversely— suited its allies. The Machel regime, while it remained an outspoken opponent of the South African state (and, during the liberation struggle in Rhodesia/Zimbabwe, highly sympathetic to ZANU), had none of Angola's appeal as a potential battleground against Western capitalist imperialism; hence, neither the South Africans nor the Soviet Bloc were willing to extend to RENAMO or FRELIMO the kinds of support that would have elevated the war to a true bid for definite control of Mozambique.

The ramifications of this strictly delineated configuration of the war were twofold. First, RENAMO cadres, far from enjoying (as UNITA did) the benefits of South African artillery support, mechanized infantry units such as 32 Battalion as a partner in joint operations, and supplies of R-1/FN-FAL rifles and other SADF-pattern war *materiel*, were only lightly equipped. This meant that they were forced to depend on arms diverted to them by the SADF from captured weapons caches seized in Angola or South Africa, or purchased on the international black market; RENAMO units were thus equipped in the same manner as their FRELIMO opponents, although in somewhat reduced quantities.[37] Second, RENAMO's missions, in keeping with this thrifty approach to its provisioning, were typically directed at economic and civilian targets. Attacks against economically sensitive targets, such as foreign aid workers, railway routes, and the Cahora Bassa hydroelectric project, were intended to cripple the Mozambican economy[38]; attacks against its civilian population were intended to demoralize the Mozambican people, render the countryside ungovernable, and strike out against specific FRELIMO policies through, for instance, the burning of communal villages.

RENAMO's objectives and lack of financial support went hand in hand with its *capacity for (and reliance on) compellence*. Forced to live off the land, RENAMO units sustained themselves through plunder and press-ganging; unable to fight government forces head-on, they settled for attacking the population on which FRELIMO depended, as is evident in this testimonial by a Mozambican civilian:

The *bandidos* like to scatter little antipersonnel mines around on paths in the villages at night, so the first person to come along in the morning stands on one ... [that's] Renamo's way of telling the *povo* [people] that Frelimo cannot protect them.[39]

At the same time, in terms of interface sovereignty, RENAMO operations were directed almost completely from a SADF special forces base at Phalaborwa, and while cadres in the field operated effectively without supervision and beyond the reach of their South African handlers, the seizure of RENAMO bases such as the one in the Gorongosa area in 1983 showed that highly specific instructions and training were given to the RENAMO leadership.[40] When conflicts of interest occurred, the South African response to this phenomenon was reportedly to assassinate any RENAMO commander whose loyalty seemed to be flagging.[41]

While RENAMO showed considerable success in destabilizing Mozambique, its true function and the core of its linkage to the South African state was made apparent between 1982 and 1983 when, following the signing of the Nkomati Accords, South Africa agreed to cease support for RENAMO on the condition that Mozambique take the same steps regarding the ANC.[42] Although some reduced levels of covert support continued to be given to RENAMO, the very idea that such a trade could be negotiated indicates the degree to which South Africa's military planners regarded their RENAMO allies as little more than bargaining chips; certainly, no equivalent repudiation of UNITA would feature in the Lusaka Accord between South Africa and Angola in the following year. What was important to the South Africans was not the partnership itself, or even that the partner ever achieve its desired outcome, but the way that the partnership could be used to turn South African military aid into Mozambican destabilization at the best possible ratio of inputs to outputs. In this regard, while the SADF-RENAMO alliance was not a gun frontier *per se*, the two clearly share a functional structure.

CONCLUSION

Table 3.1 shows a summary of the cases discussed in this chapter and the significance of the roles played by interface sovereignty and capacity for compellence in each case.

As can be seen in Table 3.1, substantial parallels connect the interstice-exploiting cases profiled in this chapter. All of the interstitial actors in

Table 3.1   Summary of cases involved in interstitial exploitation

Case	Interface sovereignty	Capacity for compellence
Gun frontier (1650–1850)	By selling guns to friendly indigenous forces in exchange for slaves, European colonial enclaves ensured their survival in the face of far larger indigenous polities and guaranteed a source of labor for plantation crops	Firearms enabled revisionist indigenous factions to destroy far larger polities than themselves, but not to implement the deterrence-based systems which would have created a new crop of threats to the Europeans
Ghazi system (1400–1826)	The *ghazi* system, including *bashi-bazouks*, corsairs and Janissaries, permitted the simultaneous valorization and marginalization of religious war and thereby made the simultaneous pursuit of security and prosperity a reality for the Ottoman empire	The *ghazis'* capacity to extract plunder and inflict painful losses on enemies within the sovereign interstice allowed them to build alliances and ensure defections of enemy forces even in the absence of formally held territory or recognized sovereignty
Petite guerre (1660–1814)	The provision of gifts of weapons and a scalp bounty by French administrators created a balance of terror across the North American continent and kept a large reserve of indigenous forces available for instant mobilization in times of war	The strategic use of cruelty by indigenous fighting forces ensured unit cohesion and smooth recruitment through the distribution of plunder, and assisted these irregular forces in eroding the confidence of militia forces that sought to oppose them
The East India Company (1700–1865)	By strategically connecting company resources and assets provided by the British state to willing partners in the decaying Mughal empire, the EIC was able to parlay a modest position on the fringe of the Asian colonial zone into holdings that granted substantial benefits to its shareholders	The absence of any organic or deeply-felt ideological connection to the long-term governance of Mughal lands left EIC forces free to deploy their capacities for violence where it would compel the most obedience, for example, along splits in political alliances where betrayal could be induced
RENAMO (1975–1992, 2013–present)	Operating with the support of would-be regional powers such as Rhodesia and South Africa, RENAMO allowed itself to become a de facto arm of their coercive regional policies while simultaneously pursuing its own rivalry with FRELIMO	RENAMO's relative lack of military capacity compared to other proxy forces (and UNITA in particular) was tailored to forcing it to emphasize terror and compellence in its operations rather than decisive victory over FRELIMO forces

question find their operation shaped by the need to provide whatever it is that their patron is deriving from the continued existence of the interstice they inhabit; furthermore, all find compellence to be the ideal tool for ensuring the continued flow of this commodity. One final thing that may be noted from this table are the durations of the partnerships profiled, which frequently run to centuries if not decades. While many aspects of the surface events attendant to interstice exploitation may resemble interstice opening (as detailed in Chap. 2) or interstice closing (as detailed in Chap. 4), these extended durations are one key sign that something different is at work. In the final analysis, an exploited interface best serves its function by simply continuing to exist.

NOTES

1. Thomas Schelling, *Arms and Influence* (USA: Yale University Press, 1966).
2. David J. Silverman, *Thundersticks: Firearms and the Violent Transformation of Native America* (USA: Harvard University Press, 2016).
3. Robin Law, "Warfare on the West African Slave Coast, 1650–1850" (103–126) in R. Brian Ferguson and Neil L. Whitehead (eds.) *War in the Tribal Zone: Expanding States and Indigenous Warfare* (Santa Fe: School of American Research Press, 1992).
4. Law (idem.) cites African trade data showing that while in the 1650s, 3 slaves could be bought for two guns, by the 1720s each slave cost 20 guns or 300 lbs of gunpowder. These figures seem good for the predator polities, but they also indicate the inherent instability of the gun frontier and the markets that it sustained.
5. Stephen P. Reyna, *Wars without End: The Political Economy of a Pre-colonial African State* (USA: University Press of New England, 1990).
6. Edward Luttwak, *The Grand Strategy of the Roman Empire: From the First Century A.D. to the Third* (Johns Hopkins University Press, 1976).
7. Douglas E Streusand, *Islamic Gunpowder Empires: Ottomans, Safavids and Mughals* (USA: Westview Press, 2011), pp. 24–26.
8. Mancur Olson, *Power and Prosperity: Outgrowing Communist and Capitalist Dictatorships* (USA: Oxford University Press, 2000).
9. Paul Wittek, *The Rise of the Ottoman Empire* (USA: Burt Franklin, 1971), p. 14.
10. Streusand, *Islamic Gunpowder Empires*, p. 80.
11. Wittek, *Rise*. Ibid.
12. Wittek, *Rise*. pp. 17–19.
13. Streusand, *Islamic Gunpowder Empires*, p. 82.
14. Wittek, *Rise*, pp. 32–36.

15. Roger Crowley, *Empires of the Sea: The Siege of Malta, the Battle of Lepanto, and the Contest for the Center of the World* (USA: Random House, 2008), p. 27.

16. Ibid. Indeed, Hayrettin Barbarossa would go from being pasha of Algiers to commanding the entire Ottoman fleet until his retirement in Istanbul in 1545.

17. J.D. DeVilliers. "The Pandour Corps at the Cape during the rule of the Dutch East India Company." The South African Military History society (June 1975). http://samilitaryhistory.org/vol033jv.html. Accessed January 24, 2019.

18. Jérôme Lacroix-Leclair and Eric Ouellet, "The Petite Guerre in New France, 1660–1759: An Institutional Analysis", *Canadian Military Journal*, Vol. 11, No. 4, Autumn 2011.

19. Stephen R. Bown, *Merchant Kings: When Companies Ruled the World, 1600–1900*, (USA: Thomas Donne Books, 2009), p. 114.

20. "The eighteenth century's golden age of legitimate privateering had its origins in the late seventeenth and early eighteenth centuries during the endemic European warfare afflicting the times and the rise of a merchant class capable of financing these ventures … [d]uring King William's War the French took the strategy a step further. When his fleet became largely bottled up, and with the expenses of major land campaigns eating up his treasury, Louis XIV permitted *armateurs* to outfit French Warships for privateering expeditions, in effect encouraging French men-of-war to cruise as privateers." Benerson Little, *The Sea Rover's Practice: Pirate Tactics and Techniques, 1630–1730* (VA: Potomac Books, 2007), p. 16.

21. Bruce Buchan "Pandours, Partisans, and Petite Guerre: The Two Dimensions of Enlightenment Discourse on War," *Intellectual History Review*, 23:3 (2013), pp. 329–347.

22. Fred Anderson, *The War that made America. A Short History of the French and Indian War*. (USA: Penguin, 2005), pp. 91–112.

23. Idem., 129–130.

24. Ironically, the end of unrestrained *petite guerre* between Europeans did not mean the end of *la guerre sauvage*. In North America after the Louisiana Purchase of 1803 and the War of 1812, what had once been a continent full of dynamic and competing colonial expansions had now become a continent full of wars of domination and pacification, as white colonists deployed unrestrained violence against indigenous forces rather than restrained violence against one other. At the same time in Europe, the Napoleonic revolutions would replace the brief heyday of more-or-less restrained conventional war with the totalizing wars of nation against nation. For a fascinating account locating the rise of totalizing war in the eighteenth century rather than the twentieth as one might think, see David

A. Bell, *The First Total War: Napoleon's Europe and the Birth of Warfare as We Know It* (USA: Houghton. Mifflin, 2007).

25. John Keay, The Honorable Company: A History of the English East India Company (UK: HarperCollins, 1993), p. 128.
26. Bown, *Merchant Kings*.
27. William Dalyrymple. March 2015. "The East India Company: The original corporate raiders." https://www.theguardian.com/world/2015/mar/04/east-india-company-original-corporate-raiders. Accessed January 24, 2019.
28. Keay, *The Honorable Company*, p. xix.
29. William Finnegan *A Complicated War: The Harrowing of Mozambique* (USA: University of California Press, 1992), p. 117.
30. Alexander Vines. *Renamo: Terrorism in Mozambique* (UK: Centre for Southern African Studies, 1991), p. 5.
31. Finnegan, *A Complicated War*, p. 69. Anti-communists, of course, immediately drew a parallel between FRELIMO and the Khmer Rouge, who were forcibly returning Cambodia to an agrarian existence around the same time.
32. JoAnn McGregor. "Violence and social change in a border economy: War in the Maputo hinterland, 1984–1992," *Journal of Southern African Studies*, March 1998, Vol. 24, Issue 1, pp. 37–61.
33. James Turner. *A Continent Ablaze: The Insurgency Wars in Africa, 1960 to the Present* (South Africa: Jonathan Ball, 1998), pp. 129–130. RENAMO continued to be known as the MNR or MNRA until 1979.
34. Hilton Hamann, *Days of the Generals: The untold story of South Africa's apartheid-era military generals* (South Africa: Struik Publishers, 2007), p. 105.
35. Finnegan, *A Complicated War*, p. 79.
36. Finnegan, *A Complicated War*, p. 74.
37. Peter Stiff, *The Silent War: South African Recce Operations 1969–1994* (UK: Galago Publishing, 1999), p. 376.
38. Joseph Hanlon, *Beggar Your Neighbors: Apartheid Power in Southern Africa* (USA: Indiana University Press, 1986); William Minter, *Apartheid's Contras: An Inquiry into the Roots of War in Angola and Mozambique* (South Africa: Witwatersrand Press, 1994).
39. Finnegan, *A Complicated War*, p. 97.
40. Turner, *Continent Ablaze*, pp. 135–136.
41. Finnegan, *A Complicated War*, p. 79. Admittedly, the fact that RENAMO retained Alfonse Dhlakama as its head all the way through its relationship with South Africa indicates that this practice, if it existed at all, was not widespread at higher levels.
42. Stiff, *The Silent War*, pp. 380–381.

CHAPTER 4

Interstice Closers

The previous two chapters explored the creation and maintenance of interstices by states wishing to derive military or economic benefits from circumventing conventional sovereign jurisdictions. In this chapter, I am concerned with states' attempts to close interstices, thereby returning the interstitial area to the formal governance of a single sovereign state. To do so, I explore four cases of interstice-closing actors at work throughout history: the Order of Malta in the Caribbean (1651–1665), the Hessian system (1676–1798), the Toyota Wars (1971–1996), and the antifascist partisan (1936–1945). As in previous chapters, I use two key characteristics as diagnostic indices and statements of functional structure concerning these interstice closers: these are fungible sovereignty and recourse to the personal, and I define them next before proceeding to the first case.

Before proceeding to these definitions, however, it bears highlighting that states have many formal or direct options when it comes to closing sovereign interstices. For example, a simple financial transaction, legal verdict, or land swap can convince a rival whose contesting claim on a piece of territory has produced a sovereign interstice, to abandon that claim. Libyan attempts to gain recognition over the Aouzou Strip under international law, discussed in the Toyota Wars case ahead, fit this model, as do the Louisiana Purchase of 1803 and the Heligoland–Zanzibar Treaty by which British territories in the North Sea were exchanged for German possessions in modern day Kenya, Tanzania, and Namibia.

© The Author(s) 2020
D. Craig, *Sovereignty, War, and the Global State,*
https://doi.org/10.1007/978-3-030-19886-2_4

Beyond the legal, financial, or boundary-redrawing arenas, states have also had recourse (for most of human history), to the "final argument of kings"—military occupation, conquest, and annexation. It is no accident that the list of exterminated polities in Europe bears as many names as it does. These dead states, once independent polities falling under the interstitial shadow of a more powerful neighbor, now live on as provinces or regions in the larger states that closed these interstices through military action.

However, such formal exercises of the rights and institutions of states are not the focus of this chapter. Instead, the four cases explored here show what happens when states go outside of their formal institutions, bringing in non-state actors to close an interstice on their behalf. Sometimes, these partnerships are embarked upon precisely to complement ongoing formal attempts, as Libya's parallel pursuit of the Aouzou Strip by legal verdict and illegal military partnership with Chadian rebels during the Toyota Wars once again shows. On other occasions, however, and especially when no legal claim exists and the costs of trading for or seizing the interstice are judged too high, the interstitial partnership represents the complete strategy of patron state. Regardless of this distinction, and as observed in the previous two chapters, we see strong common threads running through all cases of attempted interstice closure by non-state partnerships. I refer to two of these key characteristics of interstice closers as <u>fungible sovereignty</u> and <u>recourse to the personal</u>.

Fungibility refers to the ability to be changed from one form to another; <u>fungible sovereignty</u>, therefore, refers to a form of sovereignty that can easily be reconfigured or made compatible with the more conventional systemic sovereignty exhibited by states. Fungible sovereignty is a key characteristic of interstice closers because when states use their formal powers to transfer territories to one another, the forms of sovereign control that underpin their rule are compatible and transferable by default: a different flag is run up on the flagpole, and different uniforms are seen on members of the constabulary, but even if the laws that sovereignty imposes are very different the tools of their imposition are at least analogous. But as we saw in the previous two chapters, interstitial actors can have very different criteria for what counts as "rule," and may build very different institutions for broadcasting their rule than a state would. This makes it a common concern for interstice closers and their patrons—that nothing be done to complicate the eventual transfer of the interstice to the patron state. Sovereign fungibility can include, but must also go beyond, the simple mimicry exhibited by rebel militiamen who refer to themselves as "generals"; rather, the non-state must actually be built (or coerced to operate) in ways which facilitate their territory's eventual integration into the sovereign configuration exhibited by their patron.

Recourse to the personal, on the other hand, refers to the way that interstice closers are able to use the fact that they are led by individual persons, rather than by institutionalized bureaucracies, to bridge the gap between ostensibly incompatible geopolitical entities and thereby enable specific and otherwise-impossible synergies of action. Put differently: while the entire arc of post-Medieval state formation has been the delinking of the individual and personal from the actions of states—what Weber called the *stahlhartes Gehäuse* ("steel casing") of rational and institutional existence—interstice closers perform their utility to states because they are capable of acting both institutionally and personally, shifting between these two levels as each becomes more useful in the moment. Indeed, as the following cases will show, interstice closers are less "non-states" than "sometimes, just statelike enough"; and this flexibility is inseparable, both from how they operate and how this operation serves the states that employ them.

THE ORDER OF MALTA

In 1798, a series of aggressive military campaigns and diplomatic endeavors had granted the newly founded French Republic a broadly secure front across continental Europe. Only Britain remained hostile, but by taking control of Egypt, the French forces—led by Napoleon—could be used to threaten India and achieve peace through a balance of terror. On their way to Egypt, however, a blend of clumsy negotiation and stubborn intransigence led to the French naval force invading Malta, and thus effectively ending the 800-year career of one of history's most striking interstitial actors: the Order of Malta.

The Order began its existence as the Order of St. John, or the "Knights Hospitaller": what we might today call an NGO, focusing on the provision of rest and medical assistance for Christian pilgrims traveling to Christian holy sites in the Levant. Providing such assistance outside the protective umbrella of European patrons in a range of conflict-ridden locales, in turn, required an ability to defend the order's operations with violence; and developing such a capacity for the extension and maintenance of a capacity for violence on a continental scale required the establishment of durable logistical nexuses for stores and training. In this way, the Hospitallers together with a similar but independent organization known as the Knights Templar—developed not only hard and state-like shells of fortifications and garrisons from the Western Mediterranean to the Eastern, but also the sharp and state-like implements of aggressive war: uniformed knights, legions of foot soldiers, and a command caste of skilled veterans.

The shared history of the Knights Hospitaller and the Knights Templar diverges sharply after the fall, in 1292 CE, of the Christian kingdoms constituting the eastern pole of this Trans-Mediterranean assemblage. The distinction comes down to how each order attempted to find a new raison d'etre now that Jerusalem was no longer a Christian outpost. Broadly: the Knights Templar attempted to find a place within the European society of states, focusing on developing the rudimentary banking system they had provided to pilgrims into something more ambitious; the leaders of the Order of Malta instead drew their forces back to the Cyprus, then Rhodes, and drew up plans for converting their formidable ground forces into an equally formidable naval force.

These two strategies resulted in markedly different outcomes for the two orders. By the end of the fourteenth century, the Templars had been declared heretical, their members arrested and their leadership burned at the stake, while the Hospitallers had become *corsairs*, deploying their cross-emblazoned ships throughout the Mediterranean to attack and raid the shipping and port cities of Muslim states. In this incarnation, the Hospitallers soon became an integral part of the wide-ranging conflicts between the states of Europe and the expanding Ottoman Empire, experiencing both their share of victories (such as the 1571 Battle of Lepanto) and defeats (such as the loss of Rhodes to the Ottomans in 1523).

The Hospitallers were not the only source of corsairs in the Mediterranean. Crete, for example, was a base for Venetian corsairs throughout the period, constituting such a hazard for Ottoman shipping that the island was attacked by Ottoman forces in 1644 and besieged for almost 20 years.[1] However, the Hospitallers were remarkable for the degree to which they served as partners to the state. The Hospitallers were left free to recruit soldiers and sailors within, and conduct sovereign diplomacy with, the European states; in addition, after the fall of Rhodes they were granted the island of Malta as their new Mediterranean base through a 1530 decree by the Holy Roman Emperor himself. Within the bounds of this partnership, the Order thrived. In 1651, it even added the four

Caribbean islands of Saint Barthélemy, Saint Christopher, Saint Croix, and Saint Martin to its territorial holdings, becoming for a few years not only a sovereign entity but, briefly, an imperial one.

It is inarguable that the major factors in the rise and eventual fall of the Order of Malta were Mediterranean in origin, stretching from the Crusades to Napoleon's campaign in Egypt. In this regard, the Order was simply a well-designed and self-directed weapon to be set loose in the Mediterranean as a thorn in the Ottoman Empire's side, a Christian equivalent to the interstice-exploiting *bashi-bazouks* and Barbary corsairs discussed in Chap. 3. However, the Order's brief foray into the Caribbean tells not only an interesting story about the character of this interstitial actor's interactions with states, and why these "pirates for Christ" were more than just interstice exploiters, but also provides an explanation for why the Hospitallers rose to become the Order of Malta while the Templars were exterminated. After all, by the early seventeenth century the Order was not only enjoying precisely the kinds of integration within, and support from, European states that the Templars had sought—but it was doing so from within the walls of the vast network of territorial holdings, located within European states, which had been confiscated from the Templars and seamlessly reallocated to the Hospitallers by Papal Decree. The Hospitallers had inarguably found a place for themselves in the wake of the Crusades while the Templars had not: why? The Caribbean provides our answer.

As the discussion on the great chartered companies conducted in Chap. 3 lays out, the chartered company model enjoyed a variety of successes in allowing states to exploit sovereign interstices throughout the late seventeenth and early eighteenth centuries, but these successes were neither consistent across instances of the model nor across the lifetimes of any given instance. Put differently: not every experiment with certifying the exercise of state-like powers by private mercantile concerns would produce a VOC (Vereenigte Oost-Indische Compagnie) or an EIC (East India Company), nor were these two entities—arguably representing the apogee of the chartered company between them—always as successful as they, at the height of their powers, came to be. This is certainly true of France's experiments in using chartered companies to advance the state's interests in the Americas, in which the Order of Malta would play a small part.

As with its pursuit of *petit guerre* a century later, France's actions in the West Indies during the seventeenth century were both linked to, but of secondary importance to, the relative security of the French home front. In the early part of the century, with Cardinal Richelieu promoting an outward-looking French foreign policy, chartered companies such as the *Compagnie de Saint-Christophe* and its successor, the *Compagnie des Îles de l'Amérique*, were granted royal charters to expand French colonial possessions in the Caribbean, secure the sugar and tobacco trades from those waters, and extend Catholicism to the indigenous inhabitants. Eight colonial settlements were created in the shadow of the Spanish hegemony of the time and, as discussed in Chap. 2, French governors and privateers made heavy use of interstitial warfare in order to defend these tiny enclaves.

By the middle of the century, however, France had pressing European concerns to attend to, not limited to the Thirty Years' War and the internecine domestic rebellions known as the Fronde. These, combined with the failure of the chartered companies to turn a profit, left the French foreign ministry under Cardinal Mazarin looking for a way to offload its conflict-ridden Caribbean liabilities and refocus on continental affairs. The solution came in the form of the Order of Malta, which in 1651 purchased four of the eight islands from France. But this transaction would have been impossible without the particular figure of Phillippe de Longvilliers de Poincy, a high-ranking knight of the Order who had also been serving as the Lieutenant-Governor of Saint Christopher for the *Compagnie*.

Poincy's record as a faithful servant of France was, charitably put, somewhat inconsistent. Upon arriving in St. Kitts in 1638, he had after all declared the Order of Malta, not France, as the sovereign power; and in 1644, when the French state sent Noël Patrocle de Thoisy to the Caribbean replace him, Poincy at first refused to allow Thoisy to land and then had him arrested. At any other time and place in French history, Poincy's actions may have led him, the Order, and the Caribbean to a very different fate. But the French state turned out to be much more interested in filling its coffers than chasing down rogue company governors, and when Poincy was able to convince the Order's grandmaster to offer a substantial payment for half of the company's holdings, he was not only able to avoid any consequences for his acts but indeed to continue as governor of the Order's new Caribbean holdings until 1660.

During his time in office, Poincy ably defended and even expanded French interests in Caribbean, settling land disputes with the Dutch and English, deploying naval and ground forces to retake colonial settlements lost both to the actions of European states and indigenous revolts, and even founding the soon-to-be-notorious pirate haven of Tortuga as a means of keeping the peace between Catholics and the French Huguenot privateers that were to be found throughout the Caribbean during this period.[2]

At the same time, his tendency to ignore France's nominal sovereignty over the region continued to provoke conflict. When Charles de Montmagny, the former governor of New France, was dispatched from France to ensure that Poincy's rule accorded with France's interests, Poincy froze him out from all discussions of governance; the envoy died on his plantation in 1657 without ever successfully constraining Poincy's policies.

However, despite Poincy's firm grip the Order's formal existence as an imperial power in the Caribbean was nonetheless short-lived. In 1665, with France's continental fortunes on an upswing for the time being and the Order lagging behind in its payments for the four islands, the entire parcel was sold back to the French state and used to form the assets of a new chartered company with a 40-year mandate: the *Compagnie Française des Indes Occidentales.*

Stepping back from this story reveals three elements of interest concealed within the Order's albeit brief tenure in the Caribbean.

First, the Order's failure to build a durable foothold for itself in the Caribbean once more underscores the relative weaknesses of the mercantilist paradigm versus a properly configured predatory liberalism (as displayed in the operation of the EIC) for creating interstices hospitable to non-state intermediaries. In this regard, the Order joined a long list of more or less catastrophically failed French experiments with chartered intermediaries: even the successor company to which its assets were transferred failed less than ten years later, and the company was reabsorbed by the French state.

Second, the fact that the Order was able to join that list *at all*—and then, once its tenure as a Caribbean landlord was revoked, return to its "core business model" of plundering Muslim shipping in the Mediterranean for another 150 years—is significant. This resilience sets it apart from entities such as the VOC, EIC, and Hudson's Bay Company, none of which outlasted their mandate to develop and exploit the interstice within which they operated. Such a deviation cannot by examining the Order's failure to build a durable foothold in the Caribbean in terms of what it did and how it ruled; for it was no worse or better than its peers, or indeed pre-Clive EIC, in this regard. Nor can its internal configuration, hierarchy, and inarguable familiarity with interstitial violence be the explanation, given that as argued earlier it found itself to be an effective custodian of the ineffective plan that was mercantilist expansion in the seventeenth-century Caribbean.

Instead, it is most productive to attribute the Order's longevity to its capacity to project what I referred to at the outset of this chapter as <u>fungible sovereignty</u> By electing, in the wake of the fall of the last Crusader stronghold, to be (Hospitaller) corsairs rather than (Templar) landholders, the Order selected a form of non-state sovereignty which was fundamentally compatible with the state system while remaining outside it. The Templars, on the other hand, flew too close to the sun: in attempting to embed themselves within the state system, they simply became potential rivals to its larger and more powerful inhabitants. Poincy's bombast with regard to proclaiming Order sovereignty notwithstanding, the Order stepped in where and when its state patrons needed it to, and made no sovereign claims (nor created any sovereign institutions) which it could not uproot when necessary, and always paid its bills both in naval manpower and ready cash; in other words, they did nothing to the interstice that would make it truly difficult for the French state to reclaim it if necessary.

Third, in terms of the key characteristics of the Order's tenure in the Caribbean we see the salience of the Order's <u>recourse to the personal</u> in explaining how it was able to serve as a (albeit temporary) custodian for French sovereignty in the area. Poincy and Lascaris, the architects of the Order's Caribbean plan, were not just pirate monks from a Mediterranean island fortress; they were also wealthy members of the French aristocracy in their own right, and the story of the Order's brief foray into Caribbean empire-building cannot be extricated from this duality.

For example, it would not be correct to say it was the Order which purchased half of the French Caribbean and *not* Poincy and Lascaris; in fact, years before the Order's formal purchase of St. Croix, Poincy had in fact already purchased it for himself and bequeathed it to the Order; for that island at least, the groundwork for the Order's takeover in 1651 was a de facto sovereign arrangement between a French aristocrat and the state. But neither would it be correct to say that this arrangement was *all* that mattered and that the Order was irrelevant. For example, those parts of the French holdings not sold to the Order in 1651 were sold to two other aristocratic families—the du Paquets and the d'Houëls—who, like Poincy, would go on to govern them until the islands were bought back and reallocated in 1665. However, these two families could not have gotten away with rusticating two separate official envoys like Poincy did, because they could not, like Poincy, weave between different sovereign incarnations: now a French aristocrat, now a Lieutenant-Governor of a

French chartered company, now a Bailiff of the Knights of Malta. The Order's recourse to the personal—its ability, through the person of Poincy, to access flexibilities of individual identity and thus a menu of institutional mantles made available by the existence of a sovereign interstice—made its rule untouchable.

THE HESSIANS

The umbrella term "Hessians" is generally used to refer to contingents of British auxiliaries drawn from the formal state forces of small German states such as Hesse-Kassel, Brunswick, and Hannover. However, the Hessians' role in American legend and hence impact on American popular culture has far outstripped their actual impact on the nation during and in the wake of the Revolutionary War. When, almost 40 years after the Revolution, Washington Irving published his "Legend of Sleepy Hollow," the figure of the "Hessian trooper ... whose head had been carried away by a cannon-ball, in some nameless battle during the Revolutionary War" (Irving 2008) needed no introduction and served dutifully as the basis for the terrifying specter who pursues Ichabod Crane. In modern contexts, likewise, "Hessian" serves as an easily invoked term of opprobrium by which those opposed to various elements of US domestic and foreign security policies intend to impart a cynical, mercenary air to those being referred to.[3] Despite almost two centuries separating these audiences, in sum, the Hessian remains a widely recognized *bête noire* whose opaque motivations and thus unarticulated antagonism to the political collective makes them innately effective as a rhetorical device.

However, in order to transcend this simply rhetorical use of the term, it should be noted that it is no accident that Irving's tale specifically locates its spectral antagonist in New York's Westchester County. The Hessians, after all, played a very particular series of roles in the American Revolution, not least as a force extender for the thinly stretched British columns—but of the region surrounding Tarry Town and Sleepy Hollow, for example, Irving notes that ... "[the] British and American line had run near it during the war; it had, therefore, been the scene of marauding, and infested with refugees, cow-boys, and all kinds of border chivalry." Westchester County was prime territory for irregular forces, in other words, and it was from civilians' experiences in zones such as this that the image of the Hessian-as-marauding-predator is derived. Marauding and skirmishing featured prominently in the military strategies of both sides, and while the

British did field a few of their own units for such purposes (e.g., light cavalry such as "Tarleton's Raiders"), the task just as often fell to the "Hessians" of Irving's story.

It thus becomes clear that a complex dynamic exists between the rhetorical and factual dimensions of the employment of Hessian troops both in the Revolutionary War and more generally. The fact that many units on both sides raided and marauded, but only the Hessians seem to bear the ongoing taint of these actions, appears to stem from the liminal or complex status Hessian and of auxiliaries in general at a time of burgeoning nationalist and anti-imperial feeling. However, a close examination of the interstice-oriented institutions which in fact made Hessian troops available to be sent to conflicts such as the American Revolution shows a productive midpoint between two unproductive poles. In fact, the Hessians were neither generic manpower-fillers in the British order of battle, nor militarized bandits turned loose on civilians as a terror weapon, but rather a specialized product of a global security system predicated on security partnerships between microstates and hegemons, and sustained by highly instrumental domestic institutions both within those microstates and between them and their patrons.

The etymology of "auxiliary" places the term's origin within the mid- to late Roman Empire. During this phase, the legions' use of tribal contingents from conquered nations had standardized into the *auxilia* system. As with the Hessians of Irving's Westchester County, the *auxilia* both arose from the politico-military frontier of Rome's wars, and constituted it; that is to say, the use of auxiliaries as an early warning system or buffer belt not only worked because of the presence of these groups on the empire's borders, but also configured these borders so that in the course of their ordinary functioning they generated potential *auxilia* by grinding down nascent national formations into a spread of divisible and co-optable factions.[4]

In the wake of the fall of Rome, then, for a state to use "auxiliaries" continued to mean that it was using ready-made military formations whose allegiance to the state's own force commander was the result of a deferred or redirected allegiance to the auxiliaries' own sovereign elsewhere. As with the Hessians, and especially after the slow ascendancy of centralized state armies over entirely private *condottieri* or navies provided by religious orders such as the Order of Malta, these formations were generally designed to supplement, not duplicate, the patron's own forces; where the Romans used the *auxilia* to provide cavalry wings to their infantry-heavy armies, European nations employed Venetian, Swiss, and Balkan auxiliaries to provide artillerists, pike men, and littoral capacity.[5]

Several commonalities and distinctions between "mercenary" and "auxiliary" thus become clear. What these figures likely (but not always) have in common is simply that they are "foreigners" relative to the armies of the state employing them; what sets them apart, on the other hand, is primarily an issue of scale, with auxiliaries operating as cohesive units or even entire armies, and mercenaries tending to operate on a much smaller scale.[6] Our standard sense of the mercenary—that is, an individual who fights for personal compensation—may well also be true of auxiliaries, but a significant difference exists in terms of the distance between the patron and the recipient of those funds. Specifically, we tend (albeit, amidst a field of exceptions!) to associate mercenaries with more-or-less direct remuneration by the patron, whereas auxiliaries might never see a single coin bearing their patron's imprint and instead simply draw regular pay from their sovereign.

In these terms, it would thus be a clear misuse of the term to refer to the Hessians of the American Revolutionary War as a "mercenary" force. These units were, after all, formally constituted formations of the state armies of Hannover, Brunswick, Hesse-Kassel, and so forth. Although they operated under the overall authority of the British crown and its field commanders, they had their own officers, their own uniforms, and their own standardized gear. In that case, how did these formal representatives of a faraway German kingdom find themselves serving in foreign wars?

The answer to this question requires an examination of the Hessians' home states. It would be difficult to overstate the degree to which states like Hesse-Kassel had, since the seventeenth century, turned the provision of troops for foreign wars into a national industry. The clearest indicator of this specialization was an enormous growth in the military sector of these states. The 16,000 troops provided by Hesse-Kassel to the British during the American Revolutionary War, for example, should be read both against the estimated 350,000 people which made up its largely agrarian population, and its standing army of 24,000 troops; thus, that Hesse-Kassel's contribution to the American Revolutionary War approached 5% of the entire population and two thirds of its standing army.[7] One in four households in Hesse-Kassel was a military household; income from the *soldatenhandel* constituted, by some accounts, up to half of the state's foreign revenue.[8] Brunswick and the other German kingdoms had placed themselves in a similar situation, contributing forces of between 1000 (from the relatively small kingdom of Anhalt-Zerbst) and 6000 troops (Brunswick) to the British force. Each kingdom could anticipate, in exchange for the provision of these troops, to not only receive payment in advance but also to have the troops' transport and upkeep paid for by the British; a compensation for every Hessian killed in battle would also be delivered. For Hesse-Kassel alone, the contract for providing troops in North America was worth 20 million thaler or £4 million.

Providing auxiliaries, then, was not just a profitable business; it was the lifeblood of the otherwise-poor Hessian states in domestic terms, and as such, it was served by a range of carefully designed institutions. Hesse-Kassel, for example, was less of a "state with an army" than an "army-sustaining state"; conscription was universal, foreigners were widely press-ganged, and only the practitioners of essential trades—meaning, in principle, trades connected to the military—were exempt from the draft. To keep the army fed between deployments, the very administrative boundaries of the state were redrawn by Frederick II so that each canton, or district, could be tasked with the upkeep and maintenance of its own regiment: this, in combination with the payment of annual retainers by states like Britain (which paid £250,000 to keep 12,000 Hessians ready for action from 1760) enabled the Hessian states to sustain a level of militarization way in excess of any actual need.

In sum, then, the Hessian *soldatenhandel* should be understood as a system operating on two levels. Internationally, the Hessian states were able to play the game of international relations by offering their forces to allies and patrons, and ensure a steady flow of foreign revenue into their empty state coffers while doing so; and internally, they used carefully crafted military institutions to produce the raw material—professional soldiers—of the *soldatenhandel*.

Although Hessians were only one of a range of auxiliaries available to European states in the seventeenth and eighteenth centuries,[9] they were inarguably some of the most conspicuously used. Table 4.1 illustrates the breadth of Hesse-Kassel's—the most prolifically deployed of the Hessian states—deployments during this period:

If the arguments presented earlier made clear the degree to which "the Hessians needed war" during this period, Table 4.1 is intended to make clear the degree to which "seventeenth and eighteenth century war needed Hessians." Of particular note should be columns 2 and 3, "Hiring power" and "Target power," in which the hegemonic powers of Europe are over-represented. Hessian forces, in other words, were not relegated to side-

Table 4.1 Hesse-Kassel deployments in Europe, 1676–1798[a]

Conflict/Hessian deployment	Hiring power	Target power	Did hiring power win?
Scanian War, 1676–1679	Denmark, Brandenburg	France, Sweden	No
Morean War/War of the Holy League/Sixth Ottoman-Venetian War, 1684–1699	Venice	Ottoman Empire	Yes
Wars of the Grand Alliance (1688–1697)	Britain	France	Yes
Glorious Revolution, 1688	Holland	Britain	Yes
Jacobite Rising, 1689	Britain	France, Ireland	Yes
War of Spanish Succession (1701–1714)	Britain/Grand Alliance	France	Yes
Great Northern War (1700–1721)	Sweden	Russia, Prussia, Britain	No
War of Austrian Succession (1740–1748)	Britain	Bavaria, Austria	Yes
War of Austrian Succession (1740–1748)	Bavaria	France	No
Jacobite Uprising, 1715	Britain	Scotland/ France	Yes
Jacobite Uprising, 1745	Britain	France, Scotland	Yes
Seven Years' War (1756–1763)	Britain	France	Yes
American Revolution (1775–1783)	Britain	United States	No
Napoleonic Wars (1793–1794)	Britain	France	No
1798 Rebellion	Britain	Ireland	Yes

[a]Military History Now. June 15, 2013. Hessians for Hire- Meet the eighteenth century's Busiest 'Mercenaries'. Units. http://militaryhistorynow.com/2013/06/15/hired-guns-ten-amazing-facts-about-the-hessians/ (2014, September 25); Pesalj, Jovan, Nikola Samardžić, and Charles W. Ingrao. 2011. The Peace of Passarowitz, 1718. West Lafayette, IN: Purdue University Press; Showalter, Dennis. 2007. "Hessians: The Best Armies Money could Buy." Military History 24,7: 36–43; Simms, Brendan. 1998. "The Irish Rebellion, 1798." The Month 31,9: 376–380; McDowell, R.B. 1967. "The Protestant Nation." In The Course of Irish History, ed. T.W. Moody and F.X. Martin. Cork: The Mercier Press.)

shows or brush wars during their heyday, but rather to pivotal clashes between great powers.[10]

Two other things stand out from Table 4.1. First, the table shows perhaps the <u>last</u> instance of the medieval practice in which troops from a single state could, through overlapping treaty obligations, find themselves on <u>both</u> sides of a major conflict. Hessian contingents served on both sides of the War of Austrian Succession, although they never encountered each other on the field of battle.

Second, we must note the string of victories that Britain experienced with the aid of Hessian contingents right up until the American Revolution. The latter, given the colossal land area under British control during the eighteenth century in particular, suggests a very particular conclusion: that Hessians were not only an indispensable part of the British system of war in the seventeenth and eighteenth centuries, but that they permitted the British state to maintain sovereign imperial control of a territory far larger than its formal state organs could have garrisoned. This is interstice closing by any standard of analysis, and in the Hessian armies, we see a global system of warfighting completely specialized to closing interstices on behalf of overstretched imperial patron via a cluster of highly evolved states capable of providing an on-call, neutral, professional army for world-wide deployment at a moment's notice. I discuss these specializations later in the chapter.

Throughout this chapter, I have argued that in order to function effectively as interstice closers, interstitial actors require the capacity to operate under conditions of <u>fungible sovereignty</u> and they must have <u>recourse to the personal</u>.

In terms of the first of these criteria, the Hessians provide an interesting difference to the Order of Malta and the other interstice closers profiled here. Specifically, the fungibility of the Hessian model lay not in how they ruled interstices on behalf of a patron (for they did not), but rather in the interactions between the various institutions of the *soldatenhandel* already discussed permitted, and the sovereign agendas of the rulers of the Hessian states themselves. Ingrao (1987) and Taylor's (1994) institutional biographies of the Hessian principalities advance a surprising thesis: that the Hessians were able to fuse two social processes generally held to be mutually exclusive, that is, Enlightenment-style development of a rationalized, modern, bureaucratized state, and absolutist-style foreign militarism. Thus, as an "enlightened despot" (*aufgeklärter Absolutismus*), Landgrave Frederick II of Hesse-Kassel was able to pour funds into social programs and infrastructure at home *and* conduct constant wars abroad, without these two activities finding themselves in opposition either in terms of the national self-image or in budgetary terms.[11]

In large part, this deviation from the standard pattern[12] is attributed to the Hessian principalities' lack of attractiveness as potential sites of conquest by their neighbors, and indeed their relative obscurity in geopolitical terms: their foreign policy, in other words, could be entirely based around serving the *soldatenhandel* without any particular need to consider "actual" geopolitics such as the need for defensible frontiers or the temptations of conquest. The fungibility attached to Hessian sovereignty was therefore a domestic fungibility; the freedom to articulate the institutions of rule not around the standard European model but around one which made the provision of troops to interstitial wars both possible and profitable.

In terms of <u>recourse to the personal</u>, we again see an interesting variation brought to the table by the Hessian example. This stems from the eighteenth century's position at the end of the great era of dynastic and monarchic war, in which individual monarchs could be the heads of several states and thereby draw on a wider variety of allies and treaty partners than may seem intuitive in the rationalized and post-monarchic modern order. I discuss this more broadly in Chap. 6, but in the case of the American Revolution, for example, the British king George III was a German himself—in fact, the first of his line to speak English and, in addition to being the head of the British state, also the "Elector" (prince) of the German kingdom of Hannover. The provision of troops by Hannover, Hesse-Kassel, and many of the Hessian states more broadly to fight in "Elector George's" war was, then, only partially a case financial opportunism serving the *soldatenhandel*; it was also a perfectly standard exercise of alliance politics to a fellow German state on an interstate level, made possible by a form of monarchy in which recourse to the personal allowed dynastic heads who wished to engage in interstice closing to draw in uniquely large alliances of actors (like the Hessians) to do so.

THE TOYOTA WARS

Chad has been in a near-constant state of war over rule and resources since 1965. Between 1971 and 1994, however, this set of local conflicts also took on the character of a multipolar interstitial war, as Libya attempted to establish *de jure* control of a long-disputed border territory called the Aouzou Strip, and eight foreign powers (six African, two non-African) contributed various levels of military aid to factions caught up in the subsequent conflict. At the height of the fighting, the military tactics of one of the Chadian factions seized the attention and imagination of the Western media, when the *Front Armee du Nord* (FAN) used of a swarm of militarized Toyota pickup trucks to outmaneuver and outfight a much larger Libyan force. The hostilities in Chad were subsequently dubbed "The Toyota Wars."[13]

In this chapter, as with the Ogaden Vortex discussed in Chap. 3, the Toyota Wars will serve as the instructive case representing an entire class of conflicts occurring within available sovereign interstices. Unlike the conflict in Somalia, though, the actors engaged in the Toyota Wars sought not to prolong the existence of Chad and Libya's interstitial front, but to close it. From the Libyan side, this meant achieving (and then defending) the kind of stable regime change that would allow a Chadian head of state to formally cede the Aouzou Strip to Libya. From the (much more heterogeneous) opposing side, not only did this move by Libya commit groups like FAN to contesting any such regime change, but also to redrawing the geopolitical realities which had enabled the Libyan intervention in the first place so as to prevent a recurrence. Thanks in large part to the Toyota-mounted Chadian militias, the terms of the closure of the Aouzou Strip interstice ended up being settled in Chad's favor; although, as the persistence of other forms of conflict in the country makes clear, the end of an interstitial war does not necessarily herald the arrival of perpetual peace in its wake.

For the purposes of focusing on the interstitial dimension of Chad's half-century of conflict, six important events stand out: the Libyan invasion of the Strip (1971), subsequent battles for control over the capital city of Ndjamena (1979–1986), the accession of Idriss Deby to power as well as the final International Court of Justice ruling on the Aouzou Strip (1994), and finally the peace accords which concretized Deby's rule and represented the end of Libyan pursuit of interstitial war (1996).

These six events represent key points in the resolution of two separate *casus belli*: one internal to Chad, relating to which of several factions would control the postcolonial Chadian state, and one interstate, related to whether Libya or Chad had legal jurisdiction over the Aouzou Strip. These two sets of conflict dynamics interacted to produce the interstice in which the fighting took place. Had France's colonial administrators more effectively bridged Chad's internal divides and selected a less divisive figure to lead the first independent government, Libya would have had no purchase for its intervention in Chad; without Moammar el-Gadhafi's expansionist agenda and track record of proxy war by sponsorship (i.e., interstitial war) the Chadian struggle over the country's governance might have played out as a simple regional rebellion or civil war. But both dynamics *were* present, and consequently Chad experienced the interstitial Toyota Wars instead of whichever other futures it might have faced.

Turning first to the internal dynamic, it is no exaggeration to say that the postcolonial Chadian state inherited such unfavorable political geography at the moment of its independence, that not even the most benevolent of administrations could have prevented the conflicts that followed. These weaknesses took the form of incipient faultlines—religious, economic, ethnic, and infrastructural—running across the country, which successive failures of governance then aggravated in ways that made war of some sort essentially inevitable. Beginning with Chad's first president, Francois Tombalbaye, dictatorial rule from Ndjamena thus resulted in increasing estrangement between the populous, relatively wealthy, Christian south and the arid, poor Muslim north.

Three policies stand out in terms of creating both the sense and the reality of a divide between northern and southern Chad. The first of these was the so-called *Authenticité* campaign, through which Tombalbaye hoped to forge a sense of national unity and culture. *Authenticité* was inspired by the Zaireanization philosophy of Mobutu Sese Seko, and while its more innocuous elements (such as renaming Chad's capital from Fort-Laramie to Ndjamena) were well-received, others (such as the replacement of French administrators in the Muslim North with Chadians from the South, and the introduction of cultural rituals into civil service exams) were perceived as little more than a cover for the neopatrimonial advancement of Tombalbaye's own Sara ethnic group.

The second unpopular policy implemented by the Tombalbaye administration was the so-called National Loan. This sharp tax increase was required to pay for the *Authenticité* programs, but extensive corruption at the lower levels of the national tax collection system meant that the "loan" amplified grassroots grievances against the state, even in Sara tribal regions.[14] After government troops violently repressed a tax uprising in eastern Chad, anti-government groups (some formed by Chadians studying in Libya) began to conduct a war of insurgency across the country, and especially in the so-called BET[15] region in the north.

The third and final mistake which the Tombalbaye government made was its repeated use of purges and arrests to maintain discipline and root out challengers in the army and police. This policy squandered the goodwill of the armed forces, while doing little to stop or slow the hatching of coups and plots: Tombalbaye claimed in one interview that he had "survived more coup attempts than any other African leader."[16] His run of luck in this regard, however, would not last; and although the Chadian national army had proved strikingly ineffective in containing the revolt in the BET, it retained enough coercive power to assassinate Tombalbaye in 1975 and replace him with a junta headed by Felix Malloum (whom Tombalbaye had jailed before, in 1973).

By the time of Malloum's accession to power in Chad, Tombalbaye's mismanagement of the BET had effectively created two Chads: an unstable military government in the South, and a shifting alliance of rebel groups in the North. The largest of these was the *Front de Libération Nationale du Tchad* (FROLINAT), which would become the preeminent rebel actor in the war for the Aouzou Strip, and through which Libya would attempt to achieve a political settlement of the Aouzou Strip question by interstitial means.

Libya's motivations to seize the Aouzou Strip were the second conflict dynamic which produced the Toyota Wars. Three possible reasons underpin this motivation to meddle across the Chadian border: a search for strategic resources (especially uranium); the promotion of Moammar el-Gadhafi's broader ideological agenda; and, lastly, the pursuit of a broader set of experiments with sovereignty throughout Libya's spheres of influence.

Of these three, the search for uranium is least satisfactory as an explanation for the Libyan intervention. Strategic minerals were indeed a valuable commodity during the Cold War, and their presence was at various times leveraged and/or sought by a variety of client governments and their superpower patrons. However, Libya continued to attempt to press its legal claim to the Strip right up until the International Court of Justice's ruling in 1994, despite the fact that no uranium deposits were in fact discovered either following the 1971 Libyan occupation of the area, or subsequently. Even if uranium had been a motivator, by the height of the Toyota wars some 15 years after the initial occupation it had clearly been eclipsed by others concern.

A somewhat more plausible explanation is to depict the Aouzou Strip campaigns as an anti-imperial (and specifically anti-French), pan-Arab, or pan-Islamic project in line with el-Gadhafi's many other sponsorships or proxy wars in Africa and elsewhere.[17] Given the Malloum regime's reliance on French military support at the time of the Libyan intervention, as well as the strongly Muslim emphasis of FROLINAT and el-Gadhafi's creation of a multinational "Islamic Legion" which served in Chad (and to which Benin contributed troops), there is nothing in the Toyota Wars which specifically contradicts this idea. However, some elements of the careful timing of Libya's creation of its partnership with FROLINAT do argue against a purely ideological explanation.

The insurgency in northern Chad, as mentioned earlier, was far from stable over time: its dominant actors changed frequently as tribal factions struggled for primacy of umbrella groups like FROLINAT or splintered off to form rebel groups of their own. Instead of allying with the cephalous Tebu authority structures that had initially dominated the insurgency, the Libyans initially worked exclusively with members of a smaller and more acephalous tribal grouping—the Zaghawa. It was only after the Tebu faction gained control of FROLINAT that the Libyans began to assist them militarily. While the notion of a pan-Arab core to the intervention does explain a small part of this decision—the Tebu were not classified as "Arabs" by el-Gadhafi, whereas the Zaghawa were—a more likely explanation is that the Libyans saw the long-standing cross-border identities and ties between the Chadian Tebu, the Libyan Tebu, and Libya's own Senussi clans as more of a liability than a call to alliance. Both of these Libyan groups had been implicated in a plot against el-Gadhafi in 1972, after which many Tebu groups were in fact expelled from Libya.

The third explanation for the Libyan intervention—that of a sovereign experiment—shares some characteristics with the ideological explanation, in that Chad forms only one part of el-Gadhafi's broader project to redraw the map of Africa (broadly) and Arab Africa (specifically) through the creation of federations and unions, and later through bodies such as the Organisation of African Unity (OAU) and African Union (AU). Some of these initiatives were overt, that is, public in nature: representative initiatives include a range of proposed mergers between Libya and Egypt, Syria and Tunisia throughout the 1970s; pursuit of the chairmanship of the AU even convinced el-Gadhafi to briefly withdraw Libyan troops from their positions in Chad in 1979. To this, we can add Libya's (formal, legal) claim to the Aouzou Strip before the International Court of Justice (ICJ). Other dimensions of the Libyan project in Chad, however, were covert; by which I mean that they attempted not to redraw the formal and explicit sovereign boundaries of North Africa but rather its interstices, its alliances, and its ideological lineup.

This idea is well instantiated by what we know about Libya's relations with its Chadian partners. From the outset, Libya was prominent in grooming FROLINAT and shaping its ideology; several of the organization's early leaders (such as Abba Siddik) were radicalized while studying at Al Bayda University, in Libya, and this contributed to the strong pro-Libyan slant which would in time come to dominate FROLINAT's actions. However, Sudan was initially an equal partner in fomenting revolution in Chad, and FROLINAT had in fact been founded after a multiparty conference held in the Sudanese town of Nyala in 1966. When, in 1971, Libya and Sudan's initially cordial relations began to decline, Libya took advantage of Abba Siddik's rise in FROLINAT to direct the organization from being a primarily Sudanese proxy, to being a Libyan one. With FROLINAT converted into a willing agent of Libyan interests in Chad, and its leadership adjusted to deny Sudan an opportunity to use the Chadian civil war to further its own interests in the region, the Libyans finally had a custom-built coercive tool with which to work.

The first task to which FROLINAT was put seems to have been extortion: a letter of "understanding" granting Libya sovereignty over the Aouzou Strip and purportedly written by Chadian president Tombalbaye in 1975 was even part of the evidence which the Libyan delegation produced during the ICJ hearings on the fate of the Strip. The letter's authenticity, however, has been questioned, especially as the Libyan delegation only ever produced a photocopy of the original document, and Tombalbaye's death in 1975 has left the fact that there ever was a secret pact over Aouzou open for debate.

Extortion having failed, FROLINAT was put to the more practical use of regime change. For the bulk of the war, Libyan air units deployed from bases in Aouzou and southern Libya were used to deliver air strikes against FROLINAT's opponents; this combination of Libyan air support and Chadian ground forces proved highly effective at first, keeping opposition forces dispersed and preventing them from massing to defend the capital in 1979 and 1983.[18] At the same time, with only 10% of Chad's population living outside the far southern provinces, FROLINAT could use the largely empty terrain to evade enemy patrols and probes, ensuring high levels of survivability even when faced by superior forces. As Huk and DeRouen put it, "[g]eography to a large extent overcame problems of fractionalization, small fighting forces, and a lack of sophisticated weaponry."[19]

Despite these advantages, the Libya-FROLINAT alliance would soon find itself faced by other factions contesting control of the Chadian interstice. Sudan, having been frozen out of FROLINAT, transferred its support to Hissene Habre's FAN, the very same anti-Libyan faction whose Toyota swarms would eventually turn the tide of the war against el-Gadhafi, and by 1981, Sudanese ground and air troops were deployed to assist the FAN in invading Chad from its bases in Cameroon.[20] Gabon, Zaire, Benin, and Egypt also found Chadian factions who would accept their aid, albeit in pursuit of far less local goals than Libya and Sudan:

Gabon sent weapons to the conflict to honor its alliance with France, Egypt admitted to arming Habre as a hedge against Libyan destabilization of Sudan, and Zaire deployed 1600 troops to Chad in 1982 to support US efforts there. In the case of Zaire, these troops were even flown into the country on US military aircraft.[21]

Most importantly, the United States and France also entered the war on the side of the Chadian government. France not only wanted a pro-French leader who would protect its interests in Chad, but also wanted to defend the sphere of influence it enjoyed over the Francophone belt. The United States, on the other hand, saw the Chadian conflict primarily as a way to contain and undermine the el-Gadhafi regime; as one US official put it, "We basically jump for joy every time the Chadians ding the Libyans."[22] This anti-Libyan attitude stemmed, in part, from el-Gadhafi's explicitly anti-American stance on the world stage, but also from tensions around US-Libyan confrontations in the Gulf of Sirte, and the alleged Libyan sponsorship of trans-sovereign terror incidents such as the Lockerbie Bombings of 1987.

The specific details of the war that followed, although fascinating in their own right, lie outside the scope of this book. For our purposes, it suffices to say that despite early gains by the Libyan-backed FROLINAT forces, the entry of Libya's enemies into the interstitial fray led to a transfer of strategic initiative to the anti-Libyan forces and a string of defeats for Libya throughout the 1980s. French interventions in 1983 and 1986 succeeded in denying the rebels access to much-needed Libyan air support; while on the ground the FAN was provided with the fleets of Toyota trucks it needed to bring the fight to its enemies whether in the BET or across the border in Libya.

Meanwhile, the close association between the rebels and el-Gadhafi became an unlikely catalyst of Chadian national sentiment, provoking a wave of defections among the Libyan allies and the subsequent transfer of Libyan sponsorship from FROLINAT to a series of increasingly peripheral successor factions. Notwithstanding this, the Libyans were still forced to repeatedly reshuffle the upper echelons of their remaining proxy forces whenever the leadership seemed to be displaying too much independence in terms of prosecuting its war with the government forces.[23] By the late 1980s, Libya's sovereign experiment in Chad was clearly no longer militarily viable, and the 1994 ICJ verdict simply sealed its fate.

In terms of interstitial warfare, three things stand out from the instructive example provided by the Toyota Wars.

First, we see again see the importance of <u>fungible sovereignty</u> as an analytic tool for understanding interstitial warfare. The Libyan alliance with FROLINAT initially worked well because FROLINAT's sovereign agenda—unite the North, seize Ndjamena from the discredited postcolonial rulers, gain control of the state—was both well suited to raising popular support in Chad and exactly compatible with el-Gadhafi's intentions vis-a-vis the Aouzou Strip. This compatibility was no accident, with Libya exhibiting (from 1966 onward) clear instrumentality in its choice of Chadian partner to ensure their pro-Libyan outlook. As the sovereign agendas of the anti-government forces (including FROLINAT) changed throughout the 1970s, however, Libya found itself in a more hostile environment, with groups such as the FAN sharing some elements of its goals for the region (e.g., pan-Islamism) but not others (e.g., anti-Sudanese policy). With no group available, whose own sovereign agenda for Chad matched Libya's, and no time to groom a successor to FROLINAT, the Libyan intervention-by-proxy in the Chadian interstice was brought to a close even as its pursuit of the Strip by conventional legal means continued.

Second, and related to the first point, the importance of <u>recourse to the personal</u> in explaining these kinds of war is once more highlighted. This goes beyond simply pointing out that "individuals matter," or that perhaps without a Moammar el-Gadhafi there might not have been a Toyota War at all. Instead, in examining the key decision-makers within Chad we see that the final form of the war is uninterpretable if one does not consider the and religious and ethnic divides which crisscrossed Chad, and the degree to which these divides provided figures such as Siddik, Tombalbaye, Malloum, Habre, and Deby with multiple constituencies from which they could draw both ideological and militarizable support. It was the existence of these multiple constituencies and their accessibility to key individuals, for example, which caused Libya to transfer its support from minor Zaghawa tribal factions to the Tebu-dominated FROLINAT, and which later permitted breakaway northern warlords such as Habre and Deby to initially sustain their splinter groups existence in the face of the Libyan-backed FROLINAT forces, and then later find themselves militarily capable of holding Ndjamena against both the Libyans and their own rivals.

Lastly, the Toyota Wars provide us with an interstice-closing equivalent to the endemic and reciprocal interstice-exploiting wars of Chap. 3. In the Ogaden Vortex, multiple actors strove to keep the interstitial front open for ongoing hostilities; in the Toyota Wars, multiple actors competed to see on whose terms the interstice would be closed. Measured in terms of human casualties and destruction of national infrastructure, this may seem like an unnecessarily abstract point, but given the difficulty associated with ending interstitial wars at all (as discussed in Chap. 1), the existence of the Toyota Wars as an example of a war in which a decisive settlement was indeed reached is of no small import.

ANTIFASCIST PARTISANS

The aim of this chapter on "interstice closers" has been the same as that of the book more generally: to highlight continuities in the kinds of actor that states call on to pursue their agendas within the interstices of the sovereign order of the time. From Crusader knights in the Caribbean to Toyota-riding Chadian militia, this chapter has displayed in the actions of some denizens of the interstice and the agendas of their patrons a clear pattern: to take possession of an unruly space and either return it to the state system, or at least prevent its use by interstice exploiters and thereby keep it ordered for its some future return to that same system. Fungible sovereignty and recourse to the personal have been key elements in this task in each case; the former because it prevents the intermediaries from making any sovereign claims (and building any sovereign institutions) within the interstice that would clash with the agendas of the patrons, and the latter because both the function and the goal of the interstice-closing agent requires individuals who act through and speak on behalf of multiple institutions and thereby achieve otherwise-impossible synergies of action.

As the last instructional case in this three-chapter sequence, though, I want to address a tough case for the archetype of the interstice closer: the partisan. The partisan at first seems to be an uncomfortable match for inclusion in a trans-historical model, because the general concept of a partisan both in fiction and scholarship is quite localized around the European antifascist conflicts between 1936 and 1945; given this, what is the point of distinguishing a "partisan" from any insurgent fighter engaged in asymmetric war of liberation?

However, it is the *apparent* fixedness of the partisan and its *apparent* resistance to trans-historical analysis which mandates its inclusion as the final instructional case and bridge to the discussion concluded in the next chapter because, as I show in what follows, the degree to which "partisan" and "antifascist resistance fighter" have become coeval despite the term's longer history, has less to do with what a partisan does or who they are, than it does with their role vis-a-vis the sovereign order of their time, and the way this is picked up in the varying meanings and usage patterns surrounding the figure of the partisan.

Etymologically, the meaning of "partisan" undergoes an interesting shift around the time of the Thirty Years' War in Europe. Before this, a partisan was a long, spear-like weapon or polearm wielded by peasant troops; hence, in sixteenth-century Shakespeare we find "citizens, entering with clubs or partisans",[24] but by the eighteenth century we find "partisan" (or *partizan*) bundled together with *guerillo* and *Bandenkampfer* ("bandit fighter") in works of military doctrine focused on actions involving small mobile detachments of irregular troops operating independently of conventional armies.[25]

Units operating in this manner continued to be referred to as "partisans" here and there throughout the nineteenth century, but the term's apogee and most common association is certainly the assorted conflicts of the mid-twentieth century, in which partisans commanded the attention not only of military planners but also of scholars such as Carl Schmitt (*Theory of the Partisan*, 1963) and the performers of World War II antifascist anthems such as *La Complainte du Partisan* and *Bella Ciao*. This high point of usage, and the term's slow subsequent decline, makes for a striking graph when viewed using Google's Ngram database.[26]

Two elements of the decline of "partisan" as a meaningful term call out for explanation. First, given that the phenomenon of resistance against the superior forces of a foreign occupant was about to pick up, not wind down, as the liberation movements of the postcolonial era intersected with the accelerant forces of the Cold War, why did the term not successfully jump to being the standard nomenclature for anticolonial fighters after 1960? And secondly, given that the term originates in the very same era of *kleinkrieg* or *petit guerre* explored in Chap. 3, what is it that sets a partisan apart from the pandours, *ecorcheurs,* or skirmishers of that era?

In terms of my model, the same analytic move satisfies both questions, which is to point out that the partisans of World War II had a very specific role in respect to the sovereign interstice: to close it. "Closing" the interstice, in this sense, meant not just fighting behind enemy lines but doing so with a specific aim toward the eventual appearance of the liberating Allied forces. These forces, acting in such cases as the duly designated representatives of the sovereign order, would then rehabilitate the partisan's area of operation and prepare it for reintegration into the sovereign system.

Given the widespread carnage of the time, it may seem strange to assert that a functioning sovereign order existed at *all* between the 1936 and 1945, let alone one which could act as the point of reference for partisan activities. Certainly, this period represented a period in which the previous sovereign order was at its most fragmented; furthermore, we can see (in the images of the *Tausendjähriges Reich*,[27] on the one hand, and the Atlantic Charter of 1941) that there were at least two incompatible visions of the world order that would succeed it. But, as I discuss in a fuller but more theoretical way in Chap. 6, these images were nonetheless and fundamentally *global* in character; both sketched out a new order for the ages even if that new order still needed a great deal of work on the battlefield to make it a reality. Had World War II ended in an Axis victory, a book such as this one might have focused on Axis-backed partisans such as Subhash Chandra Bose in India or the *Ossewa Brandwag* in South Africa, and how these groups were (or were not) able to find a place in the post-war dispensation. But one way or another, there would have been a post-war sovereign system; and the key factor for parsing the contribution of partisan groups to the war whose conclusion had brought it about, would have been the degree to which they had effectively functioned as interstice closers within it.

Close attention to the partisan record in World War II makes the centrality of this role and the relative immutability of this process quite clear. Only in two cases—Albania and Yugoslavia—were the partisans able to expel the Axis forces and dictate the terms of their own succession, as it were; and in both cases, the substantial post-war role as dictators played by the heads of these two partisan armies (Enver Hoxha and Josep Tito, respectively) strongly emphasizes the degree of <u>recourse to the personal</u> required to reach the levels of partisan effectiveness needed to self-liberate without the presence of substantial sponsor forces. In all other cases, partisans either peacefully handed over their country to the liberators or, as was the case for those partisan factions in Poland and France whose ideologies were judged incompatible with those of their liberators (i.e., whose liberation projects exhibited insufficiently <u>fungible sovereignty</u>), found themselves either violently or nonviolently excluded from the post-occupation regime. Between the relative scarcity of unilateral partisan victory on one hand, and the pervasiveness of these post-victory purges on the other, lies the well-trodden path of dutiful interstice closure. This is indeed an irony: the partisans could only exist and operate because of the existence of a sovereign interstice formed by the overlap of foreign occupation by one set of state powers, and the military and ideological support provided by another set; but the *telos* of their existence in almost all cases meant destroying that interstice and peacefully accepting the loss of agency that came with their success.

This gives the partisans much more in common with the Order of Malta or the militias of the Toyota Wars, who sought to close the interstices that defined them, than with the interstice-exploiting bashi-bazouks, for whom the existence of an interstice was not only necessary but also desirable. However, it also means that the reforms conducted to the sovereign order after World War II—reforms which criminalized wars of occupation and drove states once more to more-or-less covert interstitial warfare in response—created a world in which the notion of a noble partisan preparing their homeland and rejoin the sovereign system became difficult to imagine. While the post-1945 sovereign order (as incarnated first in the Atlantic Charter and then in the United Nations) was inarguably more hostile to the colonial project than its predecessor, it stopped well short of retroactively defining all colonial possessions as invasions: and without invasions, how could resisters be partisans?

The seeming fixedness of "partisan warfare" in time and place, then, stems from the never-again-to-be-seen level of coherence between its core elements—that is, irregular fighters closing interstices—observable during the antifascist struggles of the mid-twentieth century. Before this, that is, between the term's creation around the Thirty Years' War and its resurgence in the Spanish Civil War, a so-called partisan would have been generally indistinguishable from any of a half-dozen other kinds of interstitial operator: lightly armed, mobile, existing outside of the formal jurisdiction of a state. After 1945, on the other hand, any sense that an interstitial fighter was the local functionary of a sanctified and soon-to-be-restored international sovereign order became impossible given the widening ideological divides attendant to the steadily intensifying Cold War. Only for decade or so during when both of these conditions obtained—a moment of *conceptual* interstitial overlap, to go with the geopolitical interstices in which the partisans moved—could we see the figure of the partisan most clearly. This serves to once again underscore the fact that it is impossible to understand the wars or fighters of an era without considering the sovereign orders that constitute it. A fuller theoretical exploration of this idea, and of the interplay between sovereign *interstices* and sovereign *order*, is conducted in Chap. 5.

CONCLUSION

Table 4.2 shows a summary of the cases discussed in this chapter and the significance of the roles played by <u>fungible sovereignty</u> and <u>recourse to the personal</u> in each case.

As can be seen in this table, substantial parallels connect the interstice-closing cases profiled in this chapter. All of the interstitial actors in question derived their ability to operate from the <u>fungibility</u> of the sovereign project that they were working toward. Furthermore, they also all made heavy use of their <u>recourse to the personal</u> as a way to achieve outcomes

Table 4.2 Summary of cases involved in interstitial closing

Case	Fungible sovereignty	Recourse to the personal
The Order of Malta (1651–1665)	Order operations in the Caribbean continued French policies without a break, dealing with several threats to French interests before handing possession back to the Crown in 1665.	Poincy and other knights utilized their dual positions as Order members and French aristocrats both to achieve their mandate to rule and to circumvent restrictions and oversight concerning that rule.
The Hessian system (1676–1798)	The *soldatenhandel* allowed Hessian states to redesign their internal configurations entirely, safeguarding domestic prosperity and foreign alliances while still maintaining the outward appearance of a self-sufficient state.	Dynastic alliances and their interactions with the Hessian states "enlightened despotism" paved the way for the Hessian business model by legitimating both their client base and the top-down command structure responsible for their deployments.
Toyota Wars (1971–1996)	The sovereign ambitions of FROLINAT and GUNT factions were crucial if the Libyan objectives regarding the Aouzou Strip were to be achieved.	Habre, Deby and other Chadian rebel leaders were able to mobilize armed militias based on their simultaneous leveraging of political and official identities and ethno-nationalist and religious identities.
Antifascist partisans (1936–1945)	Except where partisans were strong enough to operate independently and thus force the issue, only those partisan groups whose post-war agendas were found to complement their patrons' agendas were allowed to contribute to the post-war dispensation after the occupying troops had been expelled.	Partisans survived the creation of collaborationist states by mobilizing along substate (e.g., ideological, religious) lines; the persistence of successful partisan into post-war leadership underlines the importance of their individual personas and identities in the way that their wars concluded.

beyond the capacities of actors operating purely in the worlds of the state or the non-state. For this reason, and despite their separation by centuries and hemispheres, the Order of Malta, Hessians, warlords, and partisans discussed in this chapter share the crucial common feature that they alone, of all the interstitial actors profiled in this book, are adapted to excellent partners to states conducting interstice-closing warfare.

Looking at Table 4.2, the perceptive reader may note that the nineteenth century seems underrepresented in this chapter. This is not because interstice-closing interstitial wars did not take place in this century. In fact, the nineteenth century was full of successful interstice closings—specifically, those conducted by *filibusters*, private military adventurers operating outside of the state in the anticipation that the state would retrospectively sanction their actions if they achieved their goals. The United States, for example, owes much of its current shape to the actions of filibusters in California, Texas, and Hawaii. However, I have chosen to examine the figure of the filibuster not alongside their interstice-closing peers but rather alongside state-sponsored terrorists and drones in the chapter that follows.

This is precisely *because* the filibuster went from prominence in the interstitial wars of the nineteenth century, to not only a complete absence in the twenty-first century but also a kind of conceptual impossibility. The fall of the filibuster becomes, in other words, a tool for examining something briefly visible in the story of the partisan—the role of dynamics within the global sovereign order, in shaping and incentivizing interstitial warfare.

NOTES

1. Douglas E. Streusand, *Islamic Gunpowder Empires: Ottomans, Safavids and Mughals* (USA: Westview Press, 2011).
2. Germán Arciniegas, *Caribbean, sea of the new world* (USA: Markus Weiner, 2003), p. 191.
3. See, for example, Lloyd Green's assertion that "[President Obama] seeks to project US force around the globe, regardless of priority or magnitude of crisis, as if our military was a hybrid of cops and Hessians" (Lloyd Green, "Obama is the new Dubya." The Daily Beast, June 17, 2014).
4. Edward Luttwak, The Grand Strategy of the Roman Empire from the First Century A.D. to the Third (USA: Johns Hopkins University Press, 1976).

5. P.W. Singer, Corporate Warriors: The Rise of the Privatized Military Industry (USA: Cornell University Press, 2003).

6. A conspicuous exception to this rule of thumb being, of course, the *condottieri* of Enlightenment Italy—but these large mercenary groups were adapted to fight one another, not states as such.

7. For comparative purposes, the reader should note that Hesse-Kassel's mobilization rate during this period bore more of a resemblance to the United States in 1945 (12 million in uniform out of a population of 120 million) than it did to Britain in 1783 (121,000 in uniform out of a population of 6.4 million); and at the outset of the Revolutionary War, Hesse-Kassel's 24,000 standing troops represented *12 times* as many soldiers, per capita, as their patron.

8. Edward J. Lowell, *The Hessians and the other German Auxiliaries of Great Britain in the Revolutionary War* (USA: Harper & Brothers, 1884).

9. Even Britain, it should be noted, initially sought to contract with Empress Catherine the Great to provide 20,000 Russian "Hessians" for use in 1775, given fears that Hessians might find ethnic loyalties a hindrance when dealing with American colonists of German descent.

10. One ironic exception stands out in this regard. The small contingent of troops contributed by Anhalt-Zerbst to the British forces during the American Revolutionary War was indeed sent to the less-prominent posting of Corsica in order to free up the British garrison there to deploy to the colonies; however, no sooner had the Germans arrived in this "less prominent" posting than it was attacked by a Franco-Spanish force in what would become the Anglo-Spanish war of 1779–1783. The British, German, and Corsican troops held the island through four years of blockades and repeated assaults until relieved after the end of hostilities in 1783.

11. "British subsidy money allowed these princes to build more elaborate states, more "rational" bureaucracies, and more intensely articulated tribute-taking institutions than they might otherwise have built." Peter Taylor, Indentured to Liberty (USA: Cornell University Press, 1994), p. 257.

12. That is to say, of absolutism being antithetical to liberty and prosperity, as per Immanuel Kant's notion of Perpetual Peace.

13. Although the term strictly only applies to the late 1980s, I use this nomenclature to refer to the entire proxy war in Chad.

14. James E Collins. 2007. *Lessons from Chad: Ethnic Conflict and Economic Reorganization in Post Colonial Cultural Landscapes.* Honors Thesis (San Marcos, Texas). http://ecommons.txstate.edu/cgi/viewcontent.cgi?article= 1052&context=honorprog. Accessed January 30, 2019.

15. The "BET" draws its name from the three provinces that make up northern and eastern Chad: Borkou, Ennedi, and Tibesti.

16. Mario J. Azevedo and Emmanuel U. Nnadozie. *Chad: A Nation in Search of its Future* (USA: Westview Press, 1998).
17. Ronald Bruce St John, "The Ideology of Mu'ammar Al-Qadhdhafi: Theory and Practice," *International Journal of Middle East Studies* (1983), 15: pp. 471–490.
18. Julian Crandall Hollick, 'Civil War in Chad, 1978–82', *The World Today*, 38:7/8 (Jul.–Aug., 1982), pp. 297–304.
19. Karl R. DeRouen and Uk Heo (eds.), *Civil wars of the world: major conflicts since World War II* (ABC-CLIO, 2007), 243.
20. John Turner, *A Continent Ablaze: The Insurgency Wars in Africa, 1960 to the Present* (South Africa: Jonathan Ball, 1998).
21. H. Henderson. "Conflict in Chad, 1975 to Present: A Central African Tragedy." Seminar Paper, Marine Corps Command and Staff College, Marine Corps Development and Education Command, Quantico, VA, April 1984. http://www.globalsecurity.org/military/library/report/1984/HDH.htm. Accessed January 30, 2019.
22. John Greenwald. September 2007. "Disputes Raiders of the Armed Toyotas. Libya loses face, a base and a bomber in its war with Chad." http://www.time.com/time/magazine/article/0,9171,965563-2,00.html. Accessed January 30, 2019.
23. Millard Burr, Robert O. Collins, *Darfur: the long road to disaster* (Markus Wiener, 2008).
24. From Romeo and Juliet (1597): "Tybalt: Have at thee, coward! THEY FIGHT. ENTER THREE OR FOUR CITIZENS, WITH CLUBS OR PARTISANS. Citizens: Clubs, bills, and partisans! Strike! Beat them down! Down with the Capulets! Down with the Montagues!" (Romeo and Juliet, 1. 1. 72–73).
25. Arthur Ehrhardt, *Kleinkrieg: The German Experience with Guerilla Warfare, from Clausewitz to Hitler*, translated by Charles D. Nelson (USA: Casemate Books, 2016), p. 3.
26. Google Ngram Viewer. https://books.google.com/ngrams/interactive_chart?content=Partisan&year_start=1800&year_end=2000&corpus=15&smoothing=3&share=&direct_url=t1%3B%2CPartisan%3B%2Cc0. Accessed January 30, 2019.
27. "Thousand Year Reich".

CHAPTER 5

Exceptions, Exclusions, and Discussion

On July 4, 1894, the United States Congress passed the "Newlands Resolution," formally annexing the Kingdom of Hawaii as a US territory. In 1959, it would go from being a territory to being a full state, thereby joining several other states—especially California and Texas, but also including South Dakota and Florida—that owed their status or their final dimensions to the ostensibly illegal actions of private citizens of the United States, conducted while the state had been under the sovereign jurisdiction of a foreign power. These were the *filibusters*.

Two things about the filibusters are of particular interest to the argument advanced in this book.

First, as I discussed in Chap. 4, states have always had formal means on hand to close interstices—including, but not limited to, invasion by the regular forces of the state. Furthermore, any examination of the growth of the territorial boundaries of the United States during the nineteenth century shows that these techniques were well known and successfully used during this period. It is therefore interesting to note when (i.e., under what circumstances) the United States instead turned to ostensibly interstitial actors, such as the groups of US citizens abroad whose revolutions, coups, or territorial invasions would end up being recognized after the fact by US administrators. I say that the actions of the filibusters were "ostensibly" criminal because, as Thomson points out, although the United States had very specific (and, for their time, far-reaching) laws forbidding its citizens from engaging in private acts of military adventurism abroad,

© The Author(s) 2020
D. Craig, *Sovereignty, War, and the Global State*,
https://doi.org/10.1007/978-3-030-19886-2_5

such as the Neutrality Act of 1794, these laws were not consistently enforced. In some cases, filibusters were arrested and sanctioned; in other cases, they were not only left alone but given the tacit support of the state in advance of their actions. In these latter cases, as in Hawaii, the result of the filibusters' actions was generally a new territory for the United States.[1] This is, of course, "interstice closing"—and, as I will briefly show next, the filibusters' *modus operandi* adheres very closely to the key characteristics of interstice closers laid out in Chap. 4.

What is more striking about the filibusters than their adherence to my model, however, is their disappearance from world politics by 1945. Hawaii was the last territory added to the United States by filibusters; the military coordination between the Nazis' *Volksdeutsche Mittelstelle* ("Coordination Centre for Ethnic Germans") and ethnically German paramilitaries ahead of and alongside the Nazi occupation during World War II represents a similar apogee for the practice in Europe. In this chapter and the one that follows, I explore the fall of filibustering and the rise of drone warfare as two ways of sketching both the current state of interstitial warfare and—via a discussion of sovereign order—speculating about the future into which, like Walter Benjamin's image of Paul Klee's *Angelus Novus*, we are being irresistibly and blindly propelled.[2]

THE FILIBUSTERS

The word "filibuster" derives from the Spanish *filibustero* or the French *filibustier*, which in turn share their roots with the Dutch *vrijbuiter* or English "freebooter"—in other words, an adventurer outside the law. In fact, we have already encountered the birthplace of the *filibustier* in Chap. 4: the Caribbean island of Tortuga, which by the 1670s had become a haven for Dutch and French adventurers raiding Dutch and Spanish holdings from Curacao to Veracruz.[3] While this first generation of lawless interstitial actors disappeared along with the end of the Golden Age of Piracy in the early eighteenth century, the fact that Spanish speakers had more often found themselves as the targets rather than the sponsors of *filibustero* violence during this period goes a long way toward explaining the term's resurgence in the nineteenth century to once again identify bands of violent foreigners acting outside of Spanish law but inside Spanish territory.

Under this definition, the first nineteenth-century filibuster might well have been the recently retired third vice-president of the United States, Aaron Burr, whose alleged pursuit of private war in Florida and Mexico led to his brief arrest under treason charges in 1807. But whether or not he was the first, Burr was far from the last private citizen to propose war on behalf of the state, and to enjoy more or less formal encouragement from the state in response.

In June 1846, for example, US Army Major John Frémont had played an instrumental role in ensuring the success of the Bear Flag Revolt by US citizens against the Mexican authorities in California. While scrupulously obeying the letter of the Neutrality Act, Frémont's adroitness in switching between his two identities as a private citizen and a representative of the United States (i.e., his <u>recourse to the personal</u>) represented a clear violation of the Act's spirit, as he and various members of his expedition assisted the rebels in coordinating their logistics and in occupying various military fortifications in the area.

How long or successfully Frémont could have continued in this explicitly ambiguous manner without being forced into a fight with the Mexican forces will never be known: he was denied his only chance at a battle on June 28 and 29, after falling for an "intercepted military communication" that caused him to pull his forces back long enough for his opponents to escape without violence. Then, on July 7, the appearance of US troops from the Pacific Squadron with news that the United States and Mexico were now at war over a land dispute in Texas meant the end of the Bear Flag Revolt as an independent interstitial war. Nonetheless, for just under a month John Frémont served as the interstitial representative of a US government with a keen interest not only in grabbing Mexican territory but also in using the short-lived "Bear Flag Republic" as a means for heading off British designs in the region—even if the only modern sign of this filibuster adventure is the persistence of a version of the Bear Flag as California's state flag.

In part, Frémont's actions in California stand out from a century of other examples of filibustering because Frémont himself was a figure of such striking highs and lows. After briefly serving as the military governor of California after the Bear Flag Revolt, he was court-martialed for clashing with his superiors and discharged from the army, but was then reinstated as commander of US forces in the West during the civil war and even stood (briefly) as a presidential candidate in the 1864 election. However, Frémont was also someone who entered the interstice as the envoy of a state; more often, would-be filibusters found themselves in the opposite position, reaching out to the state from the interstice.

For an examination of this kind of filibuster, I move to the annexation of Hawaii with which I began this chapter.

HAWAII

In terms of my model of interstitial war, the US attitudes toward Hawaii during the half-century prior to the 1898 annexation clearly indicate the gradual creation of a sovereign interstice over the islands, followed by the inevitable use of filibuster action and subsequent annexation to resolve that interstice by closing it. The reason I identify this phase as being about a half-century in length is that US interests in the Kingdom of Hawaii exhibit a definite intensification between 1842 and 1849, when Secretary of State Daniel Webster used a series of official communiques to Hawaiian agents in Washington DC, and to representatives of Britain and France, to indicate that it would best suit the United States if the Kingdom remained independent of any European power.[4] At the same time in Hawaii, the Great *Mahele* ("division of lands") was instituted by King Kamehameha, which allowed foreigners to own land in Hawaii for the first time and inaugurated an era during which Hawaii served as a key site for US-owned plantation agriculture.

Tensions between the growing sugar interests and the Hawaiian monarchy led to the creation of white militias such as the "Honolulu Rifles"; at the same time, divisions in the Hawaiian monarchy provoked the 1874 Honolulu Courthouse Riot, which was only quelled through the intervention of US and UK warships in the region. Wary of further disruptions to the sugar industry, the US government dropped sugar tariffs on Hawaiian imports for 15 years in exchange for the right to establish a military base at Pearl Harbor in 1875; by 1887, official State Department policy was to use US forces to counter any further threat to US commerce or citizens in Hawaii. Abortive revolutions in 1889 and 1892, and then finally an 1893 coup by the sugar cane planters' militias, provided just this excuse.

Sanford Dole, the planters' leader, cited corruption and anti-democratic behavior on the part of the Hawaiian authorities as his excuse for taking power, and having formed a provisional government and a "Committee on Annexation" together with other expatriates, proposed the immediate annexation of the islands by the United States. With US Secretary of State John Stevens and President Harrison as allies, the proposed "Treaty of Annexation" made it all the way to the Senate before the election of Grover Cleveland resulted in its withdrawal for re-examination. The new administration was both strongly opposed to the coup and willing to publicly concede the US role in sparking it. As Cleveland himself put it:

I have not, however, overlooked an incident of this unfortunate affair which remains to be mentioned. The members of the provisional government and their supporters, though not entitled to extreme sympathy, have been led to their present predicament of revolt against the Government of the Queen by the indefensible encouragement and assistance of our diplomatic representative.[5]

The resistance of the Cleveland administration to Hawaiian annexation froze the issue for several years, during which Dole's provisional government continued to exercise de facto rule over the islands. An attempted counter-coup in 1895 provided a pretext for the temporary incarceration of Hawaiian Queen Lili'uokalani, although she was soon released and able to plead her case in Washington DC. Unfortunately for the Queen, the outbreak of the Spanish-American war re-invigorated debates around whether an island so valuable to the United States in economic and strategic, force-projection terms could responsibly be left vulnerable to conquest by the US rivals in the Pacific, and the Newlands Act was soon passed to ensure direct US rule over the Hawaiian interstice. It had taken Sanford Dole and his "Hawaiian League" five years of waiting and lobbying, but the care that the coup leaders had taken to ensure that Hawaii was in as compatible a shape as possible for the handover finally paid off, and the US flag was hoisted over the royal palace in Honolulu on August 12 of 1898.

Apart from once again showcasing the importance of fungible sovereignty and recourse to the personal in the operations of interstice closers, the Hawaiian annexation gives a better sense of why the actions of filibusters declined as precipitously as they did after the turn of the twentieth century. Specifically, as the variations in support of annexation between the Harrison, Cleveland, and McKinley administrations show, by the end of the nineteenth century, the strategic and economic benefits of expansionism via interstitial warfare, versus a commitment to the rule of law and to the spirit of republican government made the choice of whether to support filibustering a fraught one.

This is not, of course, to imply that states like the United States would never again put their weight behind factions opposed to unfriendly regimes located within the United States' sovereign interstices. In fact, it could be argued that the United States did more to subvert legitimately elected rulers after 1945, especially in Latin America, than it did in the nineteenth century and before. Rather, the element of interstice closing that states appeared to consider unpalatable as they began to cease their support for filibusters, was not the intervention itself but the acquisition which followed; in other words, not the meddling in the affairs of other states *per se*, but the extension of full sovereign control over the sites of that meddling.

The most obvious explanation for this increasing reticence to conquer through interstitial warfare is the growth of <u>authenticity</u> as a criterion for assessing the legitimacy of a polity throughout the nineteenth century. As David Bell and others have pointed out, before the nineteenth century any sense that the primary function of states in Europe was to serve as the authentic political face of "the people," rather than as the politicized personal fief of a sovereign monarch would have been misplaced.[6]

Even the revolutionary states that had notionally come into existence precisely to represent their people after the Enlightenment were not immune to this inauthenticity. If the first act of eighteenth- and nineteenth-century revolutionary state-makers was to create their state through decisive political and military action, the second was to perform the often-violent chore referred to my Italian politician and activist Massimo d'Azeglio in his 1865 quip that "*L'Italia è fatta. Restano da fare gli italiani*" ("We have made Italy. Now we must make Italians"). It should be of little surprise that throughout the nineteenth and early twentieth century, some of the worst politicides[7] of human history took place within states attempting to answer the question "who are we, and who is the state for?" Luckily, thanks to the growth of literacy and mass media in Europe during this period, it is precisely in such internally conflicted states that the arguments about whether certain tools or styles of warfare (like non-defensive war in France,[8] or the use of filibusters in the United States) are, or are not, compatible with the ongoing national narrative are most visible to modern audiences. In the case of the United States, for example, we find the novelist Mark Twain (who also opposed the annexation of Hawaii) objecting to the war in the Philippines not in terms of its illegality but in terms of its incompatibility with the American national narrative:

> There must be two Americas: one that sets the captive free, and one that takes a once-captive's new freedom away from him, and picks a quarrel with him with nothing to found it on; then kills him to get his land...
> True, we have crushed a deceived and confiding people; we have turned against the weak and the friendless who trusted us; we have stamped out a just and intelligent and well-ordered republic; we have stabbed an ally in the back and slapped the face of a guest; we have bought a Shadow from an

enemy that hadn't it to sell; we have robbed a trusting friend of his land and his liberty; we have invited clean young men to shoulder a discredited musket and do bandit's work under a flag which bandits have been accustomed to fear, not to follow; we have debauched America's honor and blackened her face before the world...

And as for a flag for the Philippine Province, it is easily managed. We can have a special one—our States do it: we can have just our usual flag, with the white stripes painted black and the stars replaced by the skull and cross-bones.[9]

Twain's adoption of the skull and crossbones image in this quote is, I believe, particularly useful in understanding the key objection he is trying to make. The skull and crossbones is after all the famous flag of piracy; and, as I will discuss in detail in Chap. 6, it is the absence of a political community (i.e., a state) to sanctify and speak for the violence inflicted by pirates that has been taken as a core element of the argument condemning them since Roman times. From the Romans until Twain, in other words, pirates—as *hostis humani generis*, the enemies of all humanity—represented a case in which violence was being inflicted without a just national interest to render it, while unpleasant, at least necessary. By placing the skull and crossbones on his "flag for the Philippine Province," Twain is specifically criticizing the degree to which the United States can or should ever engage in empire-building.

In terms of the decline of the filibuster between 1900 and 1945, then, Mark Twain stands in for a far larger population of onlookers championing authentic self-rule on two fronts: one, that states like the United States should limit their military actions to those considered authentic to the national narrative, and two, that states should respect the authentic self-rule of others by preserving rather than extinguishing it through annexation. By 1918, these principles would be codified in US President Woodrow Wilson's "Fourteen Points" speech to Congress, in which Wilson outlined frank public diplomacy and an international guarantee of "undoubted security of life and an absolutely unmolested opportunity of autonomous development" for national groups previously deprived of their independence, as the cornerstones of the post-World War order. Of course, as I have already mentioned, this is not to say either that Wilson's vision truly served as an iron constraint on violent intervention in other states during this period, or that states would cease to occasionally seek interstitial partners for this purpose, with the US military interventions in Russia and Mexico between 1916 and 1919 standing as a clear example of the former, and Japanese partnerships with Chinese warlords in Manchuria in the 1930s as a clear example of the latter.[10] But by the letter of the law of sovereign order, at least, these activities were forced into limited forms of use, relative to their overt and bald-faced nineteenth-century incarnation.

DRONES AND TARGETED KILLING

I have argued earlier that the rise of war-constraining national narratives, and their subsequent codification into sovereign order by 1945, explains the disappearance of the filibusters who had dominated interstice-closing activities up until that point. I now turn to the very different phenomenon of drone warfare (in particular) and the targeted killing of individuals by states (in general) in order to broaden this discussion of how sovereign orders constrain states' relationships with sovereign interstices.

In general, the best safeguard for individuals whose death or incarceration would provide military or political utility to some states has always been the protection of another state. This goes beyond states simply agreeing to hide vulnerable individuals from those who would kill or capture them; indeed, simply being placed under the legal custodianship of a patron state in this way has allowed vulnerable individuals from Martin Luther to Julian Assange to not only evade their enemies but also continue to annoy, offend, or threaten them.

Of course, no protection is ever complete, and the roster of individuals assassinated *despite* the protection of friendly states is both long and runs the gamut from criminals hiding under assumed identities, to high-level functionaries of the very states they were attacked in, such that Osama bin Laden was killed by US Special Forces as a fugitive within the territory of the Pakistani state, while Swedish Prime Minister Olof Palme was reportedly assassinated by agents of the South African *Apartheid* state while walking on the streets of Stockholm.

Although targeted killings (TK) of this kind are clearly a form of interstitial action by states, and individual acts or campaigns of TK could certainly be viewed as parts of broader interstice-opening or interstice-exploiting projects by the states that deploy TK, in this chapter I am interested specifically in the broad use of drone warfare in the US-led Global War on Terror since 2001.

In this war, drones are not being used to assist in *opening* interstices; we know this because, as we saw in Chap. 2, interstice-opening violence relies on the subversion of target state sovereignty by means of <u>regulative</u>

plasticity, and the deniability of the striking agents through sovereign excludability, and neither of these forms a consistent element of a war in which US drone strikes are both an avowed tactic and conducted with either the explicit (e.g., Niger, Afghanistan) or tacit (e.g., Pakistan) consent of the host state. Neither are drones being used as part of a scheme to exploit existing interstices, despite their clear advantages in capacity for compellence; because, as we saw in Chap. 3, interstice exploitation requires the practice of interface sovereignty, that is, the creation of a clear conduit for the conduction of economic, military, or commercial *profit* from the interstice back to the sponsor. I will discuss what exactly states "get" out of drone warfare presently, but for now suffice it to say that the current incarnation of drone warfare by global hegemons is hardly a get-rich-quick scheme along the lines of the EIC (East Indian Company) or a shield projected by weak states like the gun frontiers or *petite guerre* (although this may change if drone warfare becomes a more general weapon of war in future—for which, see Chap. 6).

Does this mean that by process of elimination at least, drones must be interstice closers? In fact, I would argue that the one thing that targeted killing via drones can never do, is close an interstice; if only because they exhibit none of the key characteristics possessed by interstice closers throughout the period covered in this book and explored in Chap. 4. Drone campaigns project no sovereignty, not even fungible sovereignty, although they may well count on the fungible sovereignty of the target state to permit US forces to operate a drone war "in collaboration" with local forces; and while they count on the recourse to the personal exhibited by the targets of TK—such that by striking the person of Anwar Al-Awlaki (a US citizen killed by a US drone strike in Yemen in 2011), the United States hopes to also strike Al Qaeda as a war-fighting institution in its own right—they exhibit none of their own.

At first glance, it may seem that these apparent incompatibilities between a form of warfare that is interstitial by its very nature, and the recurring uses to which interstitial warfare has been put throughout the period surveyed in this book, constitute a severe challenge to my model—if not to the notion of interstitial warfare in general, at least to the typology which orders interstitial warfare in terms of its intention to open, exploit, or close interstices. And, indeed, were my model simply a static and fixed typology, the challenge posed by drones not fitting into that typology would certainly be a problem.

However, just as with the fall of the filibusters discussed earlier, the ways that drones fail to easily fit my model can in fact be turned into points of entry for exploring the fundamental dynamism of interstitial warfare as a response to changes in sovereign order. Put differently, the ascendancy of drones tells us something about where the interstices of interstitial war come from, and drone warfare's apparent mismatch with the open/exploit/close typology advanced here in fact bespeaks a larger real-world mismatch between our current sovereign order and the military challenges it faces—just as the fall of the filibusters bespoke a clash between the capability of liberal democracies to project empires and the status of such acts vis-a-vis the national narrative.

As mentioned previously, I conduct my full discussion of the links between changing sovereign orders and interstitial war in the following (and final) chapter of this book. For now, instead, it must suffice to consider the consensus on what utility states *do* get out of wide-scale targeted killing, if it isn't the ability to close interstices.

Obviously, it is often very hard to know for sure what exactly a state "wants" by a certain action; one can only infer this by looking at the track record of the state and at which kinds of feedback from its action seems to provoke escalation and which de-escalation. In terms of drone warfare, this track record has primarily been the focus of work published by state security personnel, representatives of state armed forces, military strategists, civilian overseers of military operations, and (crucially) the and scholar-practitioners who address the deployment of TK. Although practitioners are not absent from the ongoing Mark Twain-esque legal debates[11] about whether or not targeted killing is a regulatively acceptable practice or one that is in keeping with the national narrative of the liberal-democratic states that are its most energetic proponents, they also conduct a second kind of inquiry into TK not found in the former perspective: that is, studies of its effectiveness, or utility as a form of interstitial warfare.

Such practitioner-focused studies of TK have tended to focus on what might be termed a "restricted case study" or more accurately a "single-unit" or "single-variable narrative": that is, an examination of TK's usefulness in a particular campaign or region, or the effect of a particular configuration of target characteristics (e.g., religious vs. secular orientation) in making the group more or less vulnerable to TK.

Certainly, cogent and insightful conclusions can be drawn from even these kinds of restricted study; however, insightfulness aside, such conclusions are from the outset limited in terms of their generalizability (e.g., does the fact that TK was, or was not expedient in Pakistan mean that it will, or will not, be expedient in Yemen, or Colombia?), and also (more problematically) by the way that the lack of common standards for data gathering, and the necessity for each researcher to draw their data anew from a constantly shifting pool of NGO and activist-derived data,[12] means that the conclusions of these studies are frequently contradictory. As a result, TK as a tool of counterinsurgency, that is, as a tactic to degrade the operational effectiveness of an insurgent enemy, is variously held to be effective, partially effective, effective in some contexts but not in others, ineffective, or outright counterproductive[13]; and this proliferation of conclusions does the adherents and clients of the practitioner-focused perspective very little good if their intention is to get a sense of TK as a whole, and thereby be able to judge when conditions are ripe (or not) for its expedient use.

Although no clear consensus exists on the battlefield or broader military utility of targeted killing, this is certainly not the practice's only utility, either for TK generally, or for the US drone war in particular. US President Barack Obama indicated this second use on December 8, 2011, when, in response to the charge that he was "appeasing" the US enemies, he said "Ask Osama bin Laden and the 22-out-of-30 top al Qaeda leaders who've been taken off the field whether I engage in appeasement. Or whoever is left out there, ask them about that."[14] In this statement, we see that TK also provides a way for states to signal to their allies, their constituents, and even their enemies (real or potential) that they are doing something in the face of the frequently nebulous threats encountered within the interstices into which contemporary global hegemons like the United States often find themselves thrust.

This relationship between targeted killing and regime confidence can be sought explicitly, as in the earlier quote by Obama, or it can also take a more subtle form in which targeted killing and drone strikes work in the background rather than the foreground. Using data from the Bank of Israel, for example, Zussman and Zussman showed the effects of Israel's TK policy regarding Hamas on investor confidence at the Tel Aviv stock market.[15] Their findings showed that announcements of the death of military figures, which implied progress toward the end of the conflict—were correlated with increased investor confidence. Similarly, states in the modern media-saturated world have seemingly found, in TK, a modern equivalent to the pursuit and display of grisly battle trophies, with the casualties of high-profile TK successes being used to send a message of regime assertiveness and command of the battlefield. Indeed, the televised corpses of Jonas Savimbi of Angola and Moammar el-Gadhafi of Libya lie at opposite ends of a decade (2003–2011) in which the media-driven personalization of global insurgency and the capacity of broadcast media have intersected to weave TK into government narrative at a level of intensity frequently sought, but less frequently attained, by the assassins and targeted killers—or Twain's pirates—in previous eras.

All of this suggests a very particular role for targeted killing in a world of interstitial warfare: rather than, in fact, seeking to derive anything in particular from the interstice or do anything to it, TK in general and drone warfare in particular should instead be seen as <u>management strategies</u> by which contemporary liberal democracies defer the challenge posed by the irresolvable (i.e., un-closeable) and costly reality of violent sovereign interstices, including but not limited to those interstices formed by "ungoverned spaces" and "failed states" containing enemies of the liberal democracies in question. These states find violent interstices irresolvable, in large part, both because their targets are better adapted to the networked, hybrid forms of violence facilitated by the interstice than they are,[16] but also because contemporary states find themselves constrained not only against invading these interstices using formal means, but also against reaching out to modern-day filibusters in the hope that these actors can close the interstice on their behalf.

In other words, what the rise of drones really tells us about interstitial warfare in the second decade of the twenty-first century is that while states around the world find themselves increasingly networked in ways that produce interstices, and increasingly able to project power into interstices, liberal democracies in particular have found themselves, over the last century or so, deprived of almost all the tools that they may have wished to rely on to close interstices, while authoritarian states like Russia labor under no such constraint because interstitial war in no way contradicts their national narrative. The result has been a ceding of the interstitial battlefield to the little green men and the drones—to paraphrase Yeats, truly a situation in which "The best lack all ability, while the worst / Are full of passionate adaptability."[17]

Two ways out of this difficult situation suggest themselves as far as the future of interactions between liberal democracies and dangerous interstices go. One of these is to attempt to reform the sovereign order itself; I discuss this in Chap. 6. The other is a modern equivalent to the *ghazi* system discussed in Chap. 3, which I discuss next by way of concluding this chapter.

PROXY WAR BY PROXY

The reader will recall that several layers of intermediary insulated the Ottoman state from the outside world, from the frontier raiders that surrounded the empire's outer limits to the elite Janissary slave-soldiers that served as its crack legions and the Sultan's personal defense against all threats—including rogue *ghazis*. As in 1400, when the Janissaries defended Mehmed II against Musa, modern liberal democracies thus have the option of using authoritarian states to conduct the interstice-closing warfare that they cannot or do not wish to engage in. One clear example of the best that such an arms-reach interstice-closing, or "proxy war by proxy," technique can achieve is Somalia, whose return from the state-shattering interstitial war detailed in Chap. 2 was the result of US strategic planners operating interstitially, that is, by enabling and encouraging Ethiopia to support various Somalian factions, rather than supporting them directly.

Having essentially engineered the destruction of Somalia after the Ogaden War, Ethiopia maintained a close eye on the region in the decades which followed. This meant tracking and occasionally leading the many regional attempts aimed at reconstituting stable governance in Somalia. As many as 15 peace conferences had been held in Somalia since the fall of Barre, although only six of these are now considered to have represented serious attempts to end the fighting[18]; of these six, Ethiopia convened two.[19] As mentioned previously, a particular sticking point for the Somalian peace process was the issue of whether the new Somalian state would be more centralized around Mogadishu, or more federalized around existing factions such as those backed by Ethiopia. The Zenawi administration favored a federal approach, and specifically pushed this agenda during the Addis Ababa Conference in 1993 and the Sodere Conference in 1997.[20] In contrast, the Egyptian and Djiboutian governments favored a centralized state structure, which put them at odds with the leaders of Somaliland and the semi-autonomous Puntland and Rahanweyn Resistance Army (RRA)-administered regions. The difficulty of getting all the combatant factions to agree to either of these plans, as well as Somaliland's refusal to enter into any negotiations of rejoining Somalia, prevented a coherent peace plan from being implemented in Somalia during this time.

Following the Al Qaeda attacks in New York and Washington DC on September 11, 2001, the United States once again became an active participant in the geopolitics of the Horn. Al Qaeda's links to Somalia were an issue of particular concern to US officials, who had frozen the assets of the Somalian finance and telecommunications firm al-Barakat in early 2001 because of its suspected links to Al Qaeda.[21] In addition, US intelligence services had found links between Somali groups and the 1998 embassy bombings in Kenya and Tanzania. These factors painted Somalia as a dangerous interstice and potential staging operation for Al Qaeda, and the United States began to seek local allies capable of closing it.

One obvious ally in this regard was a group of warlords which dubbed itself the Alliance for the Restoration of Peace and Counter-Terrorism (ARPCT). The ARPCT took in an estimated $100–150,000 in CIA funding every month, but was unable to translate this into consistent strategic benefits for the United States. Fortunately for the United States, however, the regional peace solution for Somalia at the time, which favored a strong central government, was in decline, and a peace solution which more closely accorded with Ethiopia's goals was advanced to replace it. In 2004, the Transitional National Government (TNG) was dissolved and replaced by a Transitional Federal Government (TFG), which convened in Nairobi and elected Abdullahi Yusuf Ahmed as its first president. By March 2006, TFG forces (including the US-backed ARPCT) were ready to make their grab for Mogadishu. The ARPCT, encamped in and around the city, moved first; however, despite three months of intense fighting, the warlords had failed to dislodge the Islamic Court Union (ICU) militias which at that time held the city. Initiative then passed to the ICU; by mid-June, it had driven the ARPCT out of Mogadishu, with the remnant of the ARPCT forces fleeing north to Jowhar.

It was at this time that Ethiopia committed itself to the fighting in deed as well as in name. In July, Ethiopian troops entered Somalia and began advancing toward the town of Burhakaba. ICU forces, mainly mechanized infantry in weaponized pickup trucks attempted to engage the Ethiopians at Beledweyne; when this failed, they switched to harassing the column with landmines, ambushes, and mortar fire. To win, the Ethiopians had to reach Mogadishu, and take the city without rendering it unusable for the purposes of government; for the ICU to win, they needed to turn back the Ethiopians, or stir up enough nationalist sentiment that the foreign-backed TFG disintegrated. The two sides' respective strategies (a methodical advance on the capital, vs. guerilla warfare aimed at inflicting demoralizing casualties) derived from these simple win-conditions.

The first major battle of the war occurred on December 6 at the TFG's provisional capital of Baidoa. Despite intense fighting, the ICU troops failed to rout or decimate the TFG forces. With enemy troops from Puntland moving toward Mogadishu from the northwest, and three columns of TFG/Ethiopian forces closing in from the west, the ICU's forces began a rearguard action. However, the enormous differences in firepower left them few offensive options: estimates of the TFG order of battle now suggest that Ethiopia had committed almost its entire holdings of heavy weapons, tanks, and jet aircraft to the invasion. US air support, in the form of AC-130 gunships and Tomahawk cruise missiles, was also used to strike high-value targets within the ICU column, selecting these targets via high-tech targeting and cell phone intercepts provided by the Ethiopians and their allies. By December 31, the TFG had been installed in Mogadishu and the remnants of the ICU were retreating down the coast toward Kenya.

It would be a great oversimplification to say that the war in Somalia was "won" on December 31, 2008, and it would be an even more grievous misstatement to suggest that the fall of the ICU ended conflict in the country. At the time of writing, Somalia is still a country at war, with the Al-Shabaab militias that succeeded the ICU waging a terrorist war that claims hundreds of lives in the region every year. However, more cynically, at least Somalia how has a government in its capital city instead of one sheltering in Kenya; more importantly, working with Ethiopia (and also, subsequently, the African Union) to close the interstice left behind by the fall of Barre, has not only allowed US strategic planners to develop local partnerships aimed at counter-terrorism and anti-piracy initiatives, but also to provide development aid to a region whose existence outside of the state system had for some time prevented this. Weak and conflict-ridden or not, and for better or for worse, the interstice within Somalia had been closed and the country reintegrated with the formal institutions of the global sovereign system.

CONCLUSION

In this chapter, I have discussed three seemingly difficult cases for my theory of interstitial war.

Filibusters, who once formed a key element of states' interstice-closing arsenal, seemed difficult because they had vanished so abruptly from world affairs; this challenged my assertion in the Introduction that interstitial warfare displays cross-historical continuities, and that individual episodes of interstitial war are "not only linked by a string of shadowy struggles conducted in the interstices and gray zones of formalized war … but [that] their respective worlds of war are also linked by recurring characteristics among the fighters who are recruited to serve in these interstices. States have changed greatly in the last 400 years: interstitial fighters have changed far less, and the same can be said of the recurring styles in which their powerful patrons employ them to go where those patrons cannot." However, in exploring the objections to filibustering surrounding the annexation of Hawaii to the United States and connecting this to the broader social campaigns against imperialism at that time, I used the fall of the filibuster to highlight the power of shifts in sovereign order vis-a-vis states' use of interstitial war.

Drones and targeted killing, unlike filibusters, have appeared rather than disappeared in the interstitial arsenal of states in recent years. Just as with filibusters, however, these practices seemed difficult to integrate into my model; in this case, because although stand-off weapons like drones *can* be used to open, exploit, or close interstices, the largest incarnation of drone warfare currently to be found—the US-led Global War on Terror—seems neither to operate as my model would predict, nor to have shown, over time, any striking degree of success in attaining recognizable interstitial goals. In examining the utility of drone warfare more closely, though, the lack of consensus about targeted killing's *battlefield* effectiveness was contrasted by some initial reasons to consider its domestic effectiveness as a signaling mechanism and an interstice mitigation technique. This highlighted, as had the filibusters, a mismatch not between the particular case of interstitial warfare by drone and my model, but between the current sovereign order and the kinds of outcome that states can hope for from interstices.

The United States' "proxy war by proxy" in Somalia after 2001 provided the last of the three seemingly difficult cases discussed in this chapter. This case showed clear parallels with earlier uses of nested intermediaries to conduct interstitial operations by the Ottoman Empire, and hence the difficulty it represented was less of a challenge to my model as to the implications of my model for the future. Put differently, if interstitial war shows no sign of diminishing in future, and if the only way that liberal democracies can close interstices is to rely on autocracies to providing the boots on the ground—neo-Hessians, in essence—while the liberal democracies provide money, intelligence, and lethal stand-off munitions, then what does this mean for any vision of the future in which we hope for a world with fewer or even no autocracies? Is there any way out of the interstice, in other words, other than by going back to the gun frontiers?

This question, and the insights the filibuster and drone cases concerning how various interstitial war strategies may fall into or out of favor in line with structural changes in the world around them, are dealt with in Chap. 6.

NOTES

1. Janice E. Thomson, *Mercenaries, Pirates and Sovereigns: State-Building and Extraterritorial Violence in Early Modern Europe* (USA: Princeton University Press, 1995), pp. 118–141.

2. "A Klee painting called Angelus Novus shows an angel looking as though he is about to move away from something he is fixedly contemplating. His eyes are staring, his mouth is open. This is how one perceives the angel of history. His face is turned towards the past. Where we perceive a chain of events, he sees one single catastrophe which keeps piling wreckage upon wreckage and hurls it in front of his feet. The angel would like to stay, awaken the dead, and make whole what has been smashed. But a storm is blowing from paradise. It has got caught in his wings with such violence that the angel can no longer close them. This storm irresistibly propels him into the future to which his back is turned, while the debris before him grows skyward. This storm is what we call progress." Howard Eiland and Michael W. Jennins, Walter Benjamin. A Critical Life (USA: Harvard University Press, 2014).

3. Angus Konstam, The World Atlas of Pirates (USA: Lyons Press, 2010), pp. 103–105.

4. US Department of State Archive. January 2009. Annexation of Hawaii 1898. https://2001-2009.state.gov/r/pa/ho/time/gp/17661.htm. Accessed January 31, 2019.

5. By which, of course, Cleveland meant Secretary of State Stevens. For the rest of Cleveland's statement, as well as other communiques from Stevens, Dole, and others; see Office of the Historian, Bureau of Public Affairs United States Department of State. FOREIGN RELATIONS OF THE UNITED STATES, 1894, APPENDIX II, AFFAIRS IN HAWAII. https://history.state.gov/historicaldocuments/frus1894app2/ch7subch1. Accessed January 31, 2019.

6. David A. Bell, *The First Total War: Napoleon's Europe and the Birth of Warfare as We Know It* (USA: Houghton Mifflin, 2007).

7. R.J. Rummel, Death By Government (USA: Transaction Publications, 1994).

8. Bell, Idem.

9. Library of Congress, The World of 1898: The Spanish-American War. Mark Twain, https://www.loc.gov/rr/hispanic/1898/twain.html.

10. For an example of these dynamic partnerships, see Erik W. Esselstrom, "Rethinking the Colonial Conquest of Manchuria: The Japanese Consular Police in Jiandao, 1909–1937," *Modern Asian Studies*, Vol. 39, No. 1 (Feb., 2005), pp. 39–75.

11. For a representative spread of legal discussions of TK, see the papers presented at the University of Pennsylvania's 2011 conference on Targeted Killing. https://www.law.upenn.edu/institutes/cerl/conferences/targetedkilling/. See also Michael L. Gross, "Assassination and Targeted Killing: Law Enforcement, Execution or Self-Defence?" *Journal of Applied Philosophy* 23. 323 (2006).

12. For a discussion of the challenges of drawing data in this manner, see Asher Fredman, "Precision-Guided or Indiscriminate? NGO Reporting on Compliance with the Laws of Armed Conflict" (June 1, 2010). Available at SSRN: http://ssrn.com/abstract=1633412.

13. For samples of these kinds of contradictory findings, see Steven R. David, "Fatal Choices: Israel's Policy of Targeted Killing," Mideast Security and Policy Studies 51 (2002), pp. 1–25; Aaron Mannes, "'Testing The Snake Head Strategy: Does Killing or Capturing its Leaders Reduce a Terrorist Group's Activity?" Solutions 9 (2008), pp. 40–49; Mohammed Hafez and Joseph M. Hatfield, "Do Targeted Assassinations Work? A Multivariate Analysis of Israel's Controversial Tactic during Al-Aqsa Uprising," Studies in Conflict and Terrorism 29 (2006) 359–382; and Jenna Jordan, "When Heads Roll: Assessing the Effectiveness of Leadership Decapitation," Security Studies 18 (2009), pp. 719–755.

14. For a further discussion of the role of this statement in pursuing domestic political agendas, see Frank James, "Obama in no appeasing mood as he goes after Republicans," NPR "It's All Politics" Blog (December 8, 2010), accessed at http://www.npr.org/blogs/itsallpolitics/2011/12/08/143376188/obama-in-no-mood-appeasing-mood-as-he-goes-after-republicans.

15. Asaf Zussman and Noam Zussman, "Assassinations: Evaluating the Effectiveness of an Israeli Counterterrorism Policy Using stock Market Data," *Journal of Economic Perspectives* 20:2 (Spring 2006) 193–206.

16. David Kilcullen, *Out of the Mountains: The Coming Age of the Urban Guerrilla* (USA: Cambridge University Press, 2013).

17. The actual source of this quote is W.B. Yeats' poem "The Second Coming" whose first verse reads in part:

Mere anarchy is loosed upon the world,
The blood-dimmed tide is loosed, and everywhere
The ceremony of innocence is drowned;
The best lack all conviction, while the worst
Are full of passionate intensity.

18. These six conferences were the Djibouti Talks (1991), the Addis Ababa National Reconciliation Talks (1993), the Sodere Conference (1996–1997), the Cairo Conference (1997), the Arta Peace Conference (2000), and the Mbagathi Conference (2002–2004).
19. Conciliation Resources. Working Together for Peace. 2010. http://www.c-r.org/our-work/accord/somalia/diplomacy-failed-state.php. Accessed January 31, 2019.
20. Ken Menkhaus, Hassan Sheikh, Ali Joqombe, Pat Johnson, A History of Mediation in Somalia since 1988, Center for Research and Dialogue. 2018. Interpeace. International Organization for Peacebuilding. http://www.interpeace.org/pdfs/A_History_of_Mediation_in_Somalia_0609.pdf. Accessed January 31, 2019.
21. Roland Marchal. February 2007. http://hornofafrica.ssrc.org/marchal/printable.html. Accessed January 31, 2019.

CHAPTER 6

The Dynamic Sovereign Order

Throughout this book, I have referred to interstitial war as existing outside of a "sovereign order" such that, for example, the point of the US-Ethiopian interstitial war partnership after 2009 was to return the state of Somalia to its place in the contemporary sovereign order. In this chapter, I develop this idea of a sovereign order further in three ways: first, by establishing a deeper sense of what I mean by "sovereign order"; second, by laying out the ways in which the cross-historical key characteristics common to each of the three types of interstitial actor (i.e., openers, exploiters, closers) are in fact derived from the concept of a particular sovereign order; and finally, by showing how sovereign orders throughout the period covered by this book rise, fall, and replace one another, with the result that each set of reforms to the sovereign order goes on to create the interstitial battlefields of the next. I conclude by using my notion of a "dynamic sovereign order" to bring this book all the way back around to one of the works that inspired it: Janice Thomson's *Mercenaries, Pirates and Sovereigns.*

THE CHALLENGE OF DYNAMISM

Periods of geopolitical tumult often provoke attempts to investigate and describe not simply the nature of events on the ground but to look for the "big picture,"[1] that is, for an explanatory system or dynamic model that can cope with change: all things whose changes have in some way provoked the tumultuous events that we see on our own human scale.

© The Author(s) 2020
D. Craig, *Sovereignty, War, and the Global State,*
https://doi.org/10.1007/978-3-030-19886-2_6

One work written with just such a focus is Robert Gilpin's *War and Change in World Politics*, which argues that

> [i]t is worth noting .... That the natural development of any science is from static analysis to dynamic analysis ... [s]tatic theory is simpler, and its propositions are easy to prove. Unfortunately, until the statics of a field of inquiry are sufficiently well developed and one has a good grasp of repetitive processes and recurrent phenomena, it is difficult if not impossible to proceed to the study of dynamics. From this perspective, systematic study of international relations is a young field, and much of what passes for dynamics is in reality an attempt to understand the statics of interactions of particular political systems: diplomatic bargaining, alliance behavior, crisis management, etc.[2]

Despite this commitment to dynamism, the general theory of change that Gilpin advances in his own book limits itself to explaining what we might consider "moderate" change, that is, considering when states seek to revise the global hierarchy of power and/or their own place in it. Furthermore, for a work dealing with change, the book takes several fundamentally conservative positions: for example, Gilpin argues that

> [t]he fundamental nature of international relations has not changed over the millennia. International relations continue to be a recurring struggle for wealth and power among independent actors in a state of anarchy. The classic history of Thucydides is as meaningful a guide to the behavior of states today as it was when it was written.[3]

Like Gilpin, I am (in this chapter) concerned with only a subset of changing phenomena, that is, transitions between sovereign orders; and also like him, I have throughout this book taken on the conceptually conservative Clausewitzian position that

> [w]ar is nothing but a duel on an extensive scale ... an act of violence to compel our opponent to fulfil our will .... Not merely a political act, but also a real political instrument, a continuation of political commerce, a carrying out of the same by other means.[4]

If warfare is simply politics, we must recognize that, like politics, war is subject to both to conventions and to capability-related constraints concerning its location in physical space; that is, that there are physical places where states are prohibited from deploying certain kinds of political instrument, and also that there are physical places where states simply lack the capability to overcome constraints on the actual deployment of the physical assets required to conduct warfare.

Luckily for the human species, states have many peaceful ways to respond to interstices (such as the customs unions, confederations, open border policies, shared currencies, and free trade agreements discussed under John Agnew's heading of "sovereignty regimes"). This means that states turn to interstices for the purpose of violence far less often than they might otherwise; furthermore, as I have displayed in this book, there are pronounced regularities in this interstitial violence, which at the very least suggests that there are ways to restrain interstitial actors by blocking the actions of one or more of their key characteristics—or, more cynically, to restrain the sponsoring states behind those actors by bullying or bribing them in the conventional ways of state-on-state diplomacy.

However, as per Gilpin's cautions, it is important to not mislead ourselves into thinking that just because our theories about certain phenomena (e.g., interstitial war) are static, the real world is static too. For example in Chap. 1, I described the increasing incompatibility of the distinction between "interstate" and "intrastate" war to the modern world and to conflicts such as the one currently taking place in Syria. This war features both a mix of state interveners, and a shockingly diverse constellation of sub-state factions—any given combination of which could be argued to be fighting a different "war" with one another. The desire to see things through the inter/intrastate distinction, I argued, was archaic, and the distinction itself was an artifact that, although it had indeed described something important about conflict at when it came into common use at the height of the nation-state and its totalizing wars, should now be moved beyond. This is an example of real world dynamism challenging a static model, and the notion of a dynamic sovereign order is how I hope my model of interstitial war will do better than the inter/intrastate dichotomy to which it responds.

How State Systems and Jurisdiction Combine to Produce Sovereign Order

Sovereign orders, then, are those parts of state systems (i.e., the international relations superstructure) which establish the characteristics which, first, allow states to claim *jurisdictions* in physical space, and, second, which regulate the kinds of political instruments that can be deployed within those jurisdictions. Although we cannot always "see" political instruments in use, their targets—the things that states hope to affect through the exercise of their political instruments, for example, people, markets, militarily defensible positions—often do have a location in physical place or social space, and it is to these physical or social locations that systemic regulations have appended rules about which political instruments can be deployed and when.

This set of more or less formalized rules is called "sovereignty"—a term that is itself an artifact of a time in which the origin of these rights of jurisdiction was considered to be the person of the sovereign themselves. In asserting the jurisdictional claims which defined her empire, for example, Elizabeth I styled herself *Elizabetha dei gracia Anglie Francie et Hibernie Regina Fidei Defensor* ("Elizabeth, by grace of God, Queen of England, France and Ireland, Defender of the Faith"). As a more contemporary example, we have "His Excellency, President for Life, Field Marshal Al Hadji Doctor Idi Amin Dada, VC, DSO, MC, Lord of All the Beasts of the Earth and Fishes of the Seas and Conqueror of the British Empire in Africa in General and Uganda in Particular."

Although these two titles may seem very different, I would argue that the extent of their claims is quite similar, both in the mix of religious, ethnic, and geopolitical jurisdictions claimed, and in the mix of qualifications given to justify these; and while Idi Amin's claim to be "Lord of All the Beasts" may provoke skepticism in the modern reader, but it is not much more of an overstatement of fact than Elizabeth's claim to be a divinely appointed defender of the Christian faith. In fact, the only difference between the two sets of claims is how seriously each was taken by other states in the state system: and here we see that Elizabeth has the advantage, with more of her jurisdictional claims having been treated as if they were authentic, than Idi Amin's. This is not to say that they were not contested; simply that they were considered real enough by her enemies that the death of the person bearing such a title could have—indeed, did—provoke post-mortem conflicts over those jurisdictions.

This is a subtle point, but an important one, and it connects us to a far larger literature on the ability of the state system to certify—that is, recognize—the consequences of the use of certain types of political instruments, and not others. James Whitman's *The Verdict of Battle*, for example, asks a series of similarly subtle questions about implicit and explicit conventions of this kind, such as: why are battlefield outcomes ever recognized, especially after the losers in any given military clash regained their ability to fight? Or, why were monarchic elites able to not only lay claim to a monopoly on mass violence, but to successfully claim this not just in might-makes-right terms but also in terms of a kingly right to violence not shared with the common folk—that is, as *ultima ratio regum* rather than the *Senatus Populusque Romanus* ("The Senate and the People of Rome") emblazoned on the Roman legions' battle standards?

Scholars have already taken three ways forward from questions like these because the question of where state systems come from has long been of concern to IR scholars and historians, even if the specific interactions between these systems and sovereignty in particular have been assumed rather than specifically problematized as I do in this chapter. First, one can locate the origin of the reciprocities that make jurisdictional assertions within state systems possible in a "society of states," that is, in the power of positive and reciprocal social interactions around values shared between *individuals* to magnify upwards into similarly positive interactions between *states*—Chap. 4's "recourse to the personal" in reverse, as it were, but now responsible for taking jurisdictions that people find meaningful and encoding them into relations between states. Second, one can search *within* states, arguing that either a strong or a weak selection process of interstate extermination[5] will winnow collections of diversely configured states down to the ones with the most effective synergies between, say, coercion and capital; the tendency of these states to exhibit similar sovereignties would then be a natural consequence of this winnowing. Thirdly, one can find, in theories such as Robert Gilpin's or John Ikenberry's, a kind of IR *vae victis* ("let the defeated despair"), in which the sovereign rules of each incarnation of the state system are generally chosen after moments of crisis and hierarchical revision, and are chosen by the strongest states within each new order specifically because they seem most likely to prove advantageous to these victors in the long term.[6]

I consider each of these three approaches to explaining the source of state systems to be important in terms of explaining sovereign orders and the dynamisms which shift them from one incarnation to another. The necessity of explaining the dynamisms which create and destroy sovereign order is crucial because, as we see even in the three models briefly discussed earlier, very few of the sovereign conventions of one state system will continue to be recognized by its successors—regardless of whether one thinks that these conventions were emplaced by social transactions, survival of the fittest, or victor's justice. We do not, for example, still recognize the figure of a "defender of the faith" in the early twenty-first century, even if it was a completely coherent idea in the late sixteenth century and regardless of how it came to be seen as legitimate.

With all this established, then, the concept of a sovereign order can be defined as follows:

A sovereign order is the current set of reciprocal practices that establish the jurisdictional range of recognized entities within a state system. Furthermore, because (i) state societies always contain potentially revisionist actors, (ii) the practices that make up sovereign orders exist as social truths rather than physical facts and are thus always vulnerable to revision, and (iii) the capabilities states might use to defend a sovereign order are themselves political instruments and thus subject to the sovereign order, it therefore follows that a sovereign order should also be seen as both constituted by and constitutive of the coercive capacities of its participants.

ALWAYS ON THE OUTSIDE: THE INTERSTITIAL WAR ACTOR

Eric Hobsbawm's serious consideration of the mystique of the social bandit[7] and Lawrence Lessig's quip that "[e]very generation welcomes the pirates from the last"[8] point at the same basic idea: that yesterday's outlaws are today's folk heroes, and that once the contentious politics which drew a certain actor to a life of interstitial violence have become a dim memory, only the romantic echo of their resistance will remain. One might then ask: what forces exist to refill the reservoir of interstitial actors, if the natural trajectory of society's view of these banditti is to part-forget, part-sanitize them?

Partly, the answer to this question lies in the final section of this chapter, inasmuch as changes in the dominant sovereign order draw new sovereign boundaries around states, changing who is considered a subject and who an outlaw; in this manner, to adapt Lessing's quip, each generation is busily making its own new pirates as fast as it is welcoming the old ones. But while this may help us understand who becomes the new *hostis humani generis*—that is, newly marginalized groups—it does not explain how states and their sovereign order "make" these pirates. To understand this process, we must turn to the genealogy of legal attitudes to piracy, and to Roman legal scholars such as Cicero, who first called for pirates to be seen as the "common enemy of all."[9]

The legal scholars of the Classical and Ancient periods were no stranger to interactions between formal states and non-state actors from outside the sovereign order. Julius Caesar himself was, after all, captured by Mediterranean pirates and held for ransom; and before the Roman Empire existed, pirate bands were serving in the state navy of Egypt, after Pharaoh Psamtik I convinced Ionian and Carian pillagers "to take up residence in Egypt and fight with their bronze weaponry in his army."[10] For Cicero and others, however, there was still a key difference between fighting a state as opposed to a non-state, which came down to the likelihood that one's enemy might exercise restraint in the conduct of their war against you, and hence the advisability of exercising restraint in your war against them. The Romans thus set the precedent of distinguishing between the *inimicis*, or "private enemy" versus the *hostis*, or "public enemy." This distinction continued to serve as a cornerstone of legal thinking through to the seventeenth and eighteenth centuries, maintaining such a recognizable form that the legal theorists like Wolff and Vattel could reframe it using liberal Enlightenment principles such that, by Heller-Roazen's account:

> "A private enemy is a person who seeks to hurt us and takes pleasure in doing so; a public enemy makes claims against us, or refuses ours, and maintains its rights, real or pretended, by force of arms... [It] may be that a hostis wishes no ill upon his adversary, even as he seeks, according to legitimate principles ... [to defend his rights]" Not so the private enemy: his combat aims to bring harm to his antagonist. Impelled "by malice and by hatred," the inimicus, by definition, cannot be "innocent."... [both] Wolff and Vattel maintain that a public adversary must be political; more exactly, this enemy must be <u>identifiable with a state in so far as a sovereign ruler represents it</u>.[11]

In this latter regard, Wolff and Vattel had inherited another strand of earlier work on legitimate versus illegitimate combatants, notably the Italian scholar Gentili's argument:

> He is an enemy ... who has a <u>state, a senate, a treasury, united and harmonious citizens, and some basis for a treaty of peace, should matters so shape themselves</u> ... Charles Martel said of the Saracens, that although they roved about in great numbers and had leaders, camps, and standards, they were none the less [bandits] since they had no cause for war.[12]

Gentili's position was not without its opponents—Dutch legal scholars such as van Bynkershoek, for example, argued that not only had the Saracens been legitimate enemies who deserved to be treated as such, but so too were the citizens of the Barbary Coast pirate states of van

Bynkershoek's own time.[13] Nonetheless, in the line of intellectual descent stretching from Cicero, through Gentili, to Wolff and Vattel, we begin to clearly see how it is that sovereign orders "manufacture" new generations of interstitial actors. The reasoning runs, somewhat circularly, as follows.

1. When actors do not exhibit a form of sovereignty that we recognize, they must also lack the kinds of civilizing institutions that would restrain their conduct of war or permit them to make peace after war.
2. When faced by enemies who will not restrain their conduct during war, and cannot make peace, we are ourselves absolved from having to show restraint or pursue peace.
3. When we are fighting without restraint, that means that our enemy must be outsiders to our sovereign order.
4. Outsiders to our sovereign order do not exhibit a form of sovereignty that we recognize.

If this reasoning seems implausibly cynical on the part of states, the reader should reflect on Carl Schmitt's 1950 observation that "[against] partisans you can only fight like a partisan,"[14] or on the Guantanamo Bay limbo in which the "illegal combatants" of the Afghan Taliban have been confined because they are fighters from outside the sovereign order.

We thus have our answer to the question of how it is that states continue to produce new legions of interstitial actors who can be mobilized to go where state forces cannot: it is the boundaries of sovereign orders themselves that create these new actors; and every time these boundaries shift, those they exclude become outlaws by definition. It is to an assessment of such dynamism that I now turn, by way of concluding this chapter.

DYNAMISM AND SOVEREIGN ORDER

Looking back at the range of cases discussed in Chaps. 2, 3, and 4, suggests a typology of sovereign orders represented below as Table 6.1. In this table, each row identifying both the social practices from which jurisdictional authority might be derived and the coercion-capable actors to which the order could turn for its defense against revisionist threats:

The order of the row headings in this title obeys a rough chronological sequence, such that we recognize religion as a core foundation of sovereign order that generally pre-dates, for example, the nineteenth-century concept of the nation or our contemporary post-truth society.[15] Arranging

Table 6.1 Sovereign orders included in Chaps. 2, 3, and 4

Sovereign Order	Source of sovereign authority	Sovereignty instantiated in	Means of systemic self defense	Jurisdictional claims
Religion	Divine mandate	Anointed leader chosen by priest class	Legions of the faithful, motivated by piety	Wherever the faithful or their enemies are
Dynastic succession	Line of biological descent	Rightful heirs	Patrimonial links to powerful vassals	Ruler's ancestral lands
Territorial claim	Governance over physical space	Representatives of a geographically coherent ethnic group	Mutual defense of co-ethnics against outsiders	Geographic range of ethnic group
National interest	The needs of the polity	Elected representatives, diplomats	Conscription/*Levee* en masse, total war	Demarcated territorial boundaries
International institutions	Systemic recognition, for example, Montevideo Convention	Heads of state and their appointed representatives	Collective defense	Global, but limited by hegemonic spheres of influence
The "endof history"	Victory in the Cold War	Hyperpower leader and their allies	Coercive diplomacy, regime change, peacekeepers	Global
Post-truth society	Social and physical resource networks	Demagogues	Drones, Little Green Men, black sites, assassination	Variable

sovereign orders in this way suggests an interesting interplay between each sovereign order and the one preceding it, such that, for example, the anointed leader of a faith group becomes, in time, the dynastic ruler whose lands may be contested in a civil war between rival siblings regardless of faith; or the way in which "authentic" ethnic frontiers are slowly made co-eval with the nation-state as discussed in Chap. 5. However, it is not my intention to present this typology as a strict account of state formation, or to imply that states as such go abruptly and irreversibly from row to row, in lockstep, over time. Instead, I have chosen to lay this list of sovereign orders rough chronological sequence because of the way that it invites us to contemplate the nebulous and gradual moments of transition (i.e., dynamism) by which sovereign orders replace one another: not abruptly at all, but by stages. I graphically represent this transition in Table 6.2.

Table 6.2 Interactions between dynamic sovereign orders

1356	1517	1648	1814	1941	1991	2016
Religion						
	Dynastic Succession					
		Territorial Claim				
			National Interest			
				International Institutions		
					The End of History	
						Post Truth

Each column of this table represents an era of history during the post-Medieval period covered by this book, with key dates serving as the column breaks. Each row, in contrast, represents the periods in which a certain cluster of social institutions served, via the self-constitutive process outlined in the definition given earlier, as the primary constitutive elements of the sovereign order of that time. In addition, each sovereign order should be considered to have a decaying arc over time, as it loses its effectiveness at constraining the actions of revisionist challengers—what Gilpin refers to as "systemic disequilibrium." Finally, even as these challengers finally succeed in implementing their new vision for the sovereign order, they must at least initially convince a sufficient number of the power-holders from the previous order to "buy in" to the new one. Hence, at any time, the world is subject to two or even three sovereign orders; the fading old order with its last few adherents, the dominant but increasingly disequilibrium of the current order, and the incipient new order(s) which seek to remedy these disequilibria. The key dates on the top row of Table 6.2 have been chosen in order to most effectively highlight this decay, as follows:

- **1356:** The "Golden Bull" resolves the conflicts between secular and religious authority by formalizing the Holy Roman Empire as a secular political entity tasked with defending Christian territory.
- **1517:** The Death of Charles V and the Protestant Reformation begin to erode the Holy Roman Empire's religiously derived mandate for rule. Subsequently, Europe experiences over a century of religious and imperial wars, generally prosecuted by dynastic ethno-territorial leaders acting on behalf of their vision of faith.

- **1648:** The Peace of Westphalia reins in religious warfare by linking the legitimate exercise of state rule to specific territory and the ethno-territorial dynasties that claim these territories. Subsequently, Europe experiences over a century of dynastic wars of succession, as rival dynastic heirs agitate their supporters to recognize some lines of descent and to repudiate others.
- **1814:** Following the Napoleonic wars, with the dynastic system of European sovereignty destroyed, a collection of elected leaders convene the Congress of Europe to rebalance European international relations in line with national interests and multipolarity. Subsequently, the world experiences over a century of warfare in colonial territories as European states rush to expand their national extractive networks and build their manufacturing sector faster than their rivals can.
- **1941:** After the unchecked industrialization and arms races of the nineteenth century and World War I have produced fascism and communism as rival ideologies to liberal democracy, the antifascist allies sign the Atlantic Charter which sketches out a post-war order in which potentially destabilizing unilateral or bilateral actions by states are replaced by collective security and intergovernmental organizations. However, the superpowers themselves are exempted from most of these constraints, and subsequently the world experiences 50 years of nuclear rivalry and proxy war as the superpowers build rival blocs of client states.
- **1991:** The collapse of the Soviet Union ushers in what US President George Bush refers to as a "New World Order," in which international institutions like the UN and IMF, now ostensibly freed from the barriers posed by the Cold War, will extend market-driven liberal democracy throughout the former Second and Third World, while multilateral peacekeeping forces clear up the last global conflict hotspots. However, these institutions prove massively unequal to the task, and subsequently the world experiences two decades of "New Wars" in which both states and non-states that stand in opposition to the demands of liberal internationalism nonetheless leverage the international networks provided by the globalized liberal order to conduct terrorist acts, ethnic cleansing, and interstitial warfare.
- **2016:** In the United States, United Kingdom, and France, popular elections expose the electoral institutions which nominally constrain liberal-democratic state policy as being highly susceptible to foreign influence, financial pressure from oligarchs, and misinformation more generally, with the result that these states begin to retreat from

their international commitments at the same time as autocratic states like Russia and China begin to increase their levels of international involvement and alliance-building. The subsequent forms of conflict produced by this change remain to be seen.

What should strike the reader in viewing this clarification of the periodization given here, is the degree to which—as I mentioned at the outset of this chapter—"each set of reforms to the sovereign order goes on to create the interstitial battlefields of the next." The Peace of Westphalia, for example, made secular dynasties sovereign within their own lands in order to restrain the continent-wide wars fought by religiously constituted alliances over the previous century. But no sooner were these dynasties prevented from exterminating one another under a religious banner, than they turned to doing so in the name of rival heirs. This took them to the conventional battlefield, but also (and more importantly for this book) to interstitial ones as, for example, French aid flowed to Jacobite rebels in Britain and indigenous forces in North America alike during the European dynastic wars of the late seventeenth century and early eighteenth century.

The names of these wars show just how the dynasto-territorial "solution" applied at Westphalia had become its own driver of conflict: the Monmouth Rebellion, King William's War, Queen Anne's War, the War of the Austrian Succession, the War of the Spanish Succession, Yaa Asantewa's War. After Napoleon set Europe ablaze, it was imagined that sovereign orders tied to nations might produce a stabler sovereign order than one based on crowned heads, but once again the names of the wars which followed show that warfighters had simply adjusted their targets away from what was prohibited (dynastic war) to what was not (wars of nations): hence, the Franco-Prussian War, the Mexican-American War, The Sino-French War, the Sudan Campaign, the Anglo-Boer War, World Wars I and II, and so on.

CONCLUSION

The contents of this chapter represent my response to Robert Gilpin's challenge that IR scholars should favor dynamic analyses of social phenomena in international relations over static ones, when they can. The additional work required to meet this challenge has been substantial. If the static and abstract model of sovereignty favored by traditional IR analysis were a true reflection of the human experience, Chaps. 1, 2, 3, and 4 of this book would suffice for a treatment of interstitial warfare. One might sum up the core argument of that (much simpler) book as follows:

"[S]tates attempt to circumvent sovereign conventions by means of interstitial warfare, and these circumventions fall into three categories that display clear-historical patterns." However, as the exclusions and exceptions raised in Chap. 5 make clear, the world is more complex than such a simple thesis would allow; hence the pursuit of sovereign dynamics that I have conducted in this last chapter.

The fact is that, as I have shown in this chapter, the very sovereign conventions that interstice-fighters seek to avoid change a great deal from era to era. Furthermore, as the inclusion of the "post-truth" column earlier shows, I believe that we currently find ourselves on the brink of yet another epochal shift. The biggest power-holders of the previous sovereign order—the United States and its allies—are still with us, albeit in a much-reduced position compared to where they were in 1991; at the same time, a new order of post-truth demagoguery has apparently seized the reins of the sovereign order from these entities. However, If the dynamic progression of my model is a useful way of thinking about the future, we ought not to spend as much time wringing our hands about the post-truth sovereign order as we do about determining what incipient sovereign order will soon coexist with it and eventually replace it. The world of international relations presents the onlooker with a constant stream of systemic disequilibria generated by the sovereign order of the time—the "pile of debris" before Benjamin's Angel of History. It is the task of analysts who are concerned with prediction and forecasting to begin to theorize about what new sovereign order will soon appear to resolve these.

In concluding this book, I would like to return to one of the works that inspired it: Janice Thomson's *Mercenaries, Pirates and Sovereigns*. A shallow reading of my model of dynamic social orders next to Thomson's treatment of the decline of non-state violence promoted by states might suggest an incompatibility between her position and mine, given that for Thomson the decline of non-state intermediaries was an irrevocable and singular process:

> The method used in this book is historical narrative. Application of a truly comparative methodology in precluded in this instance. The "dependent variable," the elimination of nonstate violence, constitutes a single case.

Certainly, scholars do exist for whom Thomson's argument shows more-or-less substantial incompatibilities with their own accounts of violent state-non-state partnerships.[16] However, two elements of the way that *Mercenaries, Pirates and Sovereigns*' analysis is conducted, rule out any such distancing on my part.

First, I tend to read Thomson's assertions about non-state violence's "single case," earlier, within the context of the book's subtitle ("State-Building and Extraterritorial Violence in Early Modern Europe") and within the apparent focus of the introduction, theory, and conclusion chapters, which lies more with the singularity of the evolving legislative state in Europe, especially in the nineteenth century, than with the diversity of mercenaries or pirates across history. At its core, in other words, this book is <u>indeed</u> about a single case; and it is only because of its impressive scope and the compelling nature of its argument that it finds itself applied in broader contexts where it finds an imperfect fit.

Second, Thomson seems well aware of the boundaries of her singular case method, and indeed of the interesting projects that are waiting beyond these boundaries. This awareness is scattered throughout the book, but most visible in the conclusion where Thomson draws on her boundaries to delineate her own point. As one example, making a point about the inevitability of a state monopoly on violence, Thomson asks:

> What if Wallenstein had succeeded in founding a mercenary state or a pirate commonwealth had survived? In the former case, violence would have remained a market commodity and in the latter it would have been subject to direct democracy.[17]

Outside of nineteenth-century Western Europe, of course, "Wallenstein" did survive in the figure of the warlord, the gun frontier predator polity, or the neo-Hessian; and it takes no great stretch to see the existence of pirate commonwealths both at sea and on land in various contemporary problem zones. But these are outside the region that Thomson is interested in gaining a better understanding of, and hence I am inclined to take her relative lack of focus on the kinds of accommodations discussed in this book not as an assertion that there is nothing to be learned there, but as the opposite.

Accordingly, in this book I begin where Thomson leaves off, and have attempted not only to update her argument to address the widespread return of non-state actors to the interstate battlefield since the early 1990s, but also to situate her singular study of coercion-monopolizing European monarchs within a broader framework of dynamic sovereign orders in which mercenaries, pirates and interstitial fighters have always served the state, albeit in different ways. In this, I hope I have been successful.

NOTES

1. See, for example, Samuel Huntington, Clash of Civilizations and the Remaking of World Order (USA: Simon and Schuster, 1996), and "The Clash of Civilizations Revisited." *Foreign Affairs* 24 (1993): 53–59.
2. Robert Gilpin, War and Change in International Politics (USA: Cambridge University Press, 1981), p. 4.
3. Idem., p. 7.
4. Carl von Clausewitz, Vom Kriege ("On War") translated by James John Graham (London: N. Trübner, 1873), accessed at http://www.clausewitz.com/readings/OnWar1873/TOC.htm, Book 1, Chapter 1.
5. Hendrik Spruyt, "Institutional Selection in International Relations: State Anarchy as Order." *International Organization* 48 (1994): 527–557.
6. John Ikenberry, *After Victory: Institutions, Strategic Restraint, and the Rebuilding of Order after Major Wars* (USA: Princeton University Press, 2001).
7. Eric Hobsbawm, Bandits (The New Press, 2000); see also Peter Lamborn Wilson, Pirate Utopias: Moorish Corsairs & European Renegadoes (USA: Autonomedia, 1995) and Stephen Snelders, *The Devil's Anarchy* (USA: Autonomedia, 2005).
8. Lawrence Lessig, *Free culture: How Big Media Uses Technology and the Law to Lock down Culture and Control Creativity.* Accessed at http://www.free-culture.cc/freeculture.pdf (February 4, 2019).
9. Daniel Heller-Roazen, *The Enemy of All: Piracy and the Law of Nations* (NY, USA: Zone Books, 2009).
10. Benerson Little, *The Sea Rover's Practice: Pirate Tactics and Techniques*, 1630–1730 (VA: Potomac Books, 2007).
11. Idem., pp. 93–95. Emphasis added.
12. Idem., p. 107. Emphasis added.
13. Idem., p. 110.
14. Carl Schmitt, *The Theory of the Partisan: A Commentary/Remark on the Concept of the Political* (Berlin: Duncker & Humblot, 1963). English translation © Michigan State University Press, 2004. Accessed at https://www.unqualified-reservations.org/archive/carlschmitttheoryofthepartisan.pdf (February 4, 2019).
15. Lee Mcintyre, *Post-Truth* (USA: MIT Press, 2018).
16. See, for example, the collection of essays in Alejandro Colás and Brian Mabee, *Mercenaries, Pirates, Bandits and Empires: Private Violence in Historical Context* (USA: Columbia University Press, 2010).
17. Janice E. Thomson, *Mercenaries, Pirates and Sovereigns: State-Building and Extraterritorial Violence in Early Modern Europe* (USA: Princeton University Press, 1995), p. 146.

Reading List

1. Agnew, John. *Globalization and Sovereignty* (USA: Rowman and Littlefield, 2009).
2. Agnew, John. 'Sovereignty Regimes: Territoriality and State Authority in Contemporary World Politics,' *Annals of the Association of American Geographers*, 95:2 (2005), pp. 437–461.
3. Amadife, Emmanuel N. and Warhola, James W. Africa's Political Boundaries: Colonial Cartography, the OAU, and the Advisability of Ethno-National Adjustment. *International Journal of Politics, Culture, and Society*, 6:4 (Summer 1993), pp. 533–554.
4. Anderson, Fred. *The War that made America. A Short History of the French and Indian War* (USA: Penguin, 2005).
5. Arciniegas, Germán. *Caribbean, sea of the new world* (USA: Markus Weiner, 2003).
6. Atzili, Boaz and Wendy Pearlman. 'Triadic Deterrence: Coercing Strength, Beaten by Weakness,' *Security Studies*, 21:2 (2012), pp. 301–335.
7. Azevedo, Mario J. and Emmanuel U. Nnadozie. *Chad: A Nation in Search of its Future* (USA: Westview Press, 1998).
8. Bell, David A. *The First Total War: Napoleon's Europe and the Birth of Warfare as We Know It* (USA: Houghton Mifflin, 2007).
9. Blank, Stephen J. 'Imperial ambitions: Russia's Military Buildup,' *World Affairs Institute* (May/June 2015), pp. 67–75.

© The Author(s) 2020
D. Craig, *Sovereignty, War, and the Global State*,
https://doi.org/10.1007/978-3-030-19886-2

10. Bobbitt, Philip. *The Shield of Achilles: War, peace, and the course of history* (Anchor, 2007).

11. Bown, Stephen R. *Merchant Kings: When Companies Ruled the World, 1600–1900* (USA: Thomas Donne Books, 2009), p. 114.

12. Buchan, Bruce. 'Pandours, Partisans, and Petite Guerre: The Two Dimensions of Enlightenment Discourse on War,' *Intellectual History Review*, 23:3 (2013), pp. 329–347.

13. Buhaug, Halvard and Jan Ketil Rød. 'Local determinants of African civil wars, 1970–2001,' *Political Geography*, 25 (2006), pp. 315–335.

14. Burr, Millard and Robert O. Collins, *Darfur: the long road to disaster* (Markus Wiener, 2008).

15. Cameron, David R., and Mitchell A. Orenstein. 'Post-Soviet Authoritarianism: The Influence of Russia in Its "Near Abroad",' *Post-Soviet Affairs*, 28:1 (2012), pp. 1–44.

16. Canada: Immigration and Refugee Board of Canada, Somalia: Information regarding Radio Kulmis, 1 May 1990, SOM5487. https://www.refworld.org/docid/3ae6ab2448.html. Accessed 21 January 2019.

17. Cimbala, Stephen J. 'Sun Tzu and Salami Tactics? Vladimir Putin and Military Persuasion in Ukraine,' *The Journal of Slavic Military Studies*, 27:3 (21 February–18 March 2014), pp. 359–379.

18. Colás, Alejandro and Brian Mabee. *Mercenaries, Pirates, Bandits and Empires: Private Violence in Historical Context* (USA: Columbia University Press, 2010).

19. Collins, James E. *Lessons from Chad: Ethnic Conflict and Economic Reorganization in Post Colonial Cultural Landscapes.* Honors Thesis, San Marcos, Texas, 2007. http://ecommons.txstate.edu/cgi/viewcontent.cgi?article=1052&context=honorprog. Accessed 30 January 2019.

20. Craig, Dylan. '"Ultima Ratio Regum: Remix or Redux?" State Security Policy and Proxy Wars in Self-Governing Africa,' *Strategic Insights*, 9 (2010), pp. 3–37.

21. Craig, Dylan. 'Developing a Comparative Perspective on the Use of Non-States in War,' *Journal of African Security*, 4:3 (2011), pp. 171–194.

22. Crowley, Roger. *Empires of the Sea: The Siege of Malta, the Battle of Lepanto, and the Contest for the Center of the World* (USA: Random House, 2008).

23. Crummey, Donald. *Banditry, Rebellion, & Social Protest in Africa* (UK: Heinemann, 1986).
24. Dalrymple, William. March 2015. 'The East India Company: The original corporate raiders.' https://www.theguardian.com/world/2015/mar/04/east-india-company-original-corporate-raiders. Accessed 24 January 2019.
25. David, Steven R. 'Fatal Choices: Israel's Policy of Targeted Killing,' *Mideast Security and Policy Studies*, 51 (2002), pp. 1–25.
26. DeRouen, Karl R., and Uk Heo (eds.), *Civil wars of the world: major conflicts since World War II* (ABC-CLIO, 2007).
27. Deutsch, Karl W. 'Quincy Wright's Contribution to the Study of War,' in Quincy Wright, *A Study of War* (USA: University of Chicago Press, 1964).
28. DeVilliers, J.D. 'The Pandour Corps at the Cape during the rule of the Dutch East India Company,' *The South African Military History Society* (June 1975). http://samilitaryhistory.org/vol033jv.html. Accessed 24 January 2019.
29. Draper, Robert. 'Shattered Somalia,' *National Geographic*, 216:3 (September 2009), pp. 70–97.
30. Duffield, Mark. 'War as a Network Enterprise: The New Security Terrain and its Implications,' *Cultural Values*, 6:1 (2002), pp. 153–165.
31. Echevarria, Antulio J., II, 'On the Clausewitz of the Cold War: Reconsidering the Primacy of Policy in On War,' *Armed Forces & Society*, 34 (2007), p. 90.
32. Ehrhardt, Arthur. *Kleinkrieg: The German Experience with Guerilla Warfare, from Clausewitz to Hitler*, translated by Charles D. Nelson (USA: Casemate Books, 2016).
33. Eiland, Howard and Michael W. Jennins. *Walter Benjamin. A Critical Life* (USA: Harvard University Press, 2014).
34. Esselstrom, Erik W. 'Rethinking the Colonial Conquest of Manchuria: The Japanese Consular Police in Jiandao, 1909–1937,' *Modern Asian Studies*, 39:1 (Feb., 2005), pp. 39–75.
35. Fazal, Tanisha M. *State death: the politics and geography of conquest, occupation, and annexation* (USA: Princeton University Press, 2011).
36. Fernandez-Armesto, Felipe. *Civilizations* (Macmillan, 2000), pp. 137–147 and Charles, Tilly. *Coercion, Capital, and European States, AD 990–1990* (USA: Blackwell Ltd., 1990).

37. Finnegan, William. *A Complicated War: The Harrowing of Mozambique* (USA: University of California Press, 1992).
38. Fredman, Asher. 'Precision-Guided or Indiscriminate? NGO Reporting on Compliance with the Laws of Armed Conflict' (June 1, 2010). Available at SSRN: http://ssrn.com/abstract=1633412.
39. Freedman, Lawrence. 'Ukraine and the Art of Limited War,' *Survival: Global Politics and Strategy*, 56:6 (2014), pp. 7–38.
40. Gedmin, Jeffrey. 'Beyond Crimea. What Vladimir Putin Really Wants,' *World Affairs* (July/August 2014), pp. 8–16.
41. Gilpin, Robert. *War and Change in International Politics* (USA: Cambridge University Press, 1981).
42. Greenwald, John. September 2007. 'Disputes Raiders of the Armed Toyotas. Libya loses face, a base and a bomber in its war with Chad.' http://www.time.com/time/magazine/article/0,9171,965563-2,00.html. Accessed 30 January 2019.
43. Gross, Michael L. 'Assassination and Targeted Killing: Law Enforcement, Execution or Self-Defence?' *Journal of Applied Philosophy*, 23 (2006), p. 323.
44. Hafez, Mohammed and Joseph M. Hatfield, 'Do Targeted Assassinations Work? A Multivariate Analysis of Israel's Controversial Tactic during Al-Aqsa Uprising,' *Studies in Conflict and Terrorism*, 29 (2006), pp. 359–382.
45. Haines, John R. 'How, Why and When Russia Will Deploy Little Green Men – And Why the US Cannot,' *Foreign Policy Research Institute E-Note* (March 9, 2016). https://www.fpri.org/article/2016/03/how-why-and-when-russia-will-deploy-little-green-men-and-why-the-us-cannot/. Accessed 21 January 2019.
46. Hamann, Hilton. *Days of the Generals: The untold story of South Africa's apartheid-era military generals* (South Africa: Struik Publishers, 2007).
47. Hanlon, Joseph. *Beggar Your Neighbors: Apartheid Power in Southern Africa* (USA: Indiana University Press, 1986).
48. Heller-Roazen, Daniel. *The Enemy of All: Piracy and the Law of Nations* (NY, USA: Zone Books, 2009).
49. Henderson, H. Conflict in Chad, 1975 to Present: A Central African Tragedy. Seminar Paper, Marine Corps Command and Staff College, Marine Corps Development and Education Command, Quantico, VA, April 1984.

50. Hensel, Paul R. 'ISA Compendium: SSIP Data Sets.' http://www.paulhensel.org/compendium.html.   Accessed   3 February 2019.
51. Herbst, Jeffery. *States and Power in Africa: Comparative Lessons in Authority and Control* (USA: Princeton University Press, 2000).
52. Jackson, Robert H. *Quasi-states: Sovereignty, International Relations and the Third world* (UK: Cambridge University Press, 1990).
53. Hobsbawm, Eric. *Bandits* (The New Press, 2000).
54. Hollick, Julian Crandall. 'Civil War in Chad, 1978–82,' *The World Today*, 38:7/8 (Jul.–Aug., 1982), pp. 297–304.
55. Holsti, Kalevi. *The State, War, and the State of War* (Cambridge, UK: Cambridge University Press, 2001).
56. Hopkirk, Peter. *The Great Game. On Secret Service in High Asia* (UK: Oxford University Press, 1990).
57. Huggler, Justin. 'Putin Privately Threatened to Invade Poland, Romania and the Baltic States.' *Daily Telegraph*, 19 September 2014. http://www.telegraph.co.uk/news/worldnews/europe/russia/11106195/Putin-privately-threatened-to-invade-Poland-Romania-and-the-Balticstates.html. Accessed 3 February 2019.
58. Huntington, Samuel. The *Clash of Civilizations and the Remaking of World Order* (USA: Simon and Schuster, 1996), and 'The Clash of Civilizations Revisited,' *Foreign Affairs*, 24 (1993).
59. Ikenberry, John. *After Victory: Institutions, Strategic Restraint, and the Rebuilding of Order after Major Wars* (USA: Princeton University Press, 2001).
60. James, Cyril. *The Black Jacobins; Toussaint L'Ouverture and the San Domingo Revolution* (USA: Vintage Books, 1963), p. 91.
61. Jordan, Jenna. 'When Heads Roll: Assessing the Effectiveness of Leadership Decapitation,' *Security Studies*, 18 (2009), pp. 719–755.
62. Kaldor, Mary. *New and Old Wars: Organized Violence in a Global Era* (USA: Stanford University Press, 2007).
63. Keay, John. *The Honorable Company*: A History of the English East India Company (UK: HarperCollins, 1993).
64. Keesing's Record of World Events (formerly Keesing's Contemporary Archives), Volume XXIV, May, 1978 'Ethiopia, Ethiopian', Page 29706.

65. Kende, Istvan, 'Wars of Ten Years (1967–1976),' *Journal of Peace Research*, 15:3 (1978), pp. 227–241.

66. Khrushcheva, Nina. 'Inside Vladimir Putin's mind Looking Back in Anger,' *World Affairs* (July/August 2014), pp. 17–24.

67. Kilcullen, David. *Out of the Mountains: The Coming Age of the Urban Guerrilla* (USA: Cambridge University Press, 2013).

68. Marten, Kimberly. 'Putin's Choices: Explaining Russian Foreign Policy and Intervention in Ukraine,' *The Washington Quarterly*, 38:2 (2015), pp. 189–204.

69. Kittrie, Orde. *Lawfare: Law as a Weapon of War* (Oxford University Press, 2016).

70. Klikushin, Mikhail. 'Little Green Men' From Russia Are Coming – And Lithuania Isn't Prepared.' *The Observer* (04/21/17), https://observer.com/2017/04/russian-little-green-men-lithuania-invasion/. Accessed 22 January 2019.

71. Konstam, Angus. *The World Atlas of Pirates* (USA: Lyons Press, 2010).

72. Lacroix-Leclair, Jérôme and Eric Ouellet, 'The Petite Guerre in New France, 1660–1759: An Institutional Analysis,' *Canadian Military Journal*, 11:4 (Autumn, 2011).

73. Law, Robin. 'Warfare on the West African Slave Coast, 1650–1850,' in *War in the Tribal Zone: Expanding States and Indigenous Warfare*, ed. R. Brian Ferguson and Neil L. Whitehead (Santa Fe: School of American Research Press, 1992), pp. 103–126.

74. Lessig, Lawrence. *Free culture: How Big Media Uses Technology and the Law to Lock down Culture and Control Creativity*. http://www.free-culture.cc/freeculture.pdf. Accessed 4 February 2019.

75. Lewis, Ioan M. *A Modern History of Somalia* (UK: Longman, 1980).

76. Library of Congress, The World of 1898: The Spanish-American War. Mark Twain. https://www.loc.gov/rr/hispanic/1898/twain.html.

77. Linz, Juan. *Totalitarian and Authoritarian Regimes* (USA: Lynne Rienner, 2000).

78. Little, Benerson. *The Sea Rover's Practice: Pirate Tactics and Techniques, 1630–1730* (VA: Potomac Books, 2007).

79. Lowell, Edward J. *The Hessians and the other German Auxiliaries of Great Britain in the Revolutionary War* (USA: Harper & Brothers, 1884).

80. Luhn, Alec. November 2017. 'Russian soldiers' captured in Ukraine to face trial on terrorism charges. *The Guardian*. https://www.theguardian.com/world/2015/may/18/russian-soldiers-ukraine-trial-terrorism-charges. Accessed 2 February 2019.

81. Luttwak, Edward. *The Grand Strategy of the Roman Empire from the First Century A.D. to the Third* (USA: Johns Hopkins University Press, 1976).

82. Malaquias, Assis. 'Diamonds are a guerrilla's best friend: the impact of illicit wealth on insurgency strategy,' *Third World Quarterly*, 22:3 (2001), pp. 311–325.

83. Manchester, William. *A World Lit Only by Fire: The Medieval Mind and the Renaissance-Portrait of an Age* (USA: Back Bay Books, 2009).

84. Mannes, Aaron. 'Testing the Snake Head Strategy: Does Killing or Capturing its Leaders Reduce a Terrorist Group's Activity?' *Solutions*, 9 (2008), pp. 40–49.

85. Marchal, Roland. February 2007. http://hornofafrica.ssrc.org/marchal/printable.html. Accessed 31 January 2019.

86. Markakis, John. 'Nationalities and the State in Ethiopia,' *Third World Quarterly*, 11:4, Ethnicity in World Politics (Oct, 1989), pp. 118–130.

87. McChrystal, Stanley. 'It Takes a Network: The New Front Line of Modern Warfare,' *Foreign Policy* (March–April 2011).

88. McDowell, R.B. 'The Protestant Nation,' in *The Course of Irish History*, ed. T.W. Moody and F.X. Martin (Cork: The Mercier Press, 1967).

89. McGregor, JoAnn. 'Violence and social change in a border economy: War in the Maputo hinterland, 1984–1992,' *Journal of Southern African Studies*, 24:1 (March 1998), pp. 37–61.

90. Mcintyre, Lee. *Post-Truth* (USA: MIT Press, 2018).

91. Menkhaus, Ken, Hassan Sheikh, Ali Joqombe, Pat Johnson. *A History of Mediation in Somalia since 1988.* (Interpeace [International Organization for Peacebuilding]/Center for Research and Dialogue, 2018). http://www.interpeace.org/pdfs/A_History_of_Mediation_in_Somalia_0609.pdf. Accessed 31 January 2019.

92. Metz, H.C. Library of Congress. Federal Research Division & Thomas Leiper Kane Collection. (1993) Somalia: A Country Study. Washington, DC: Federal Research Division, Library of

Congress: For sale by the Supt. of Docs., U.S. G.P.O. [Pdf] Retrieved from the Library of Congress, https://www.loc.gov/item/93016246/. Accessed 3 February 2019.

93. Migdal, Joel. *State in Society: studying how states and Societies Transform and Constitute one Another* (USA: Cambridge University Press, 2001).

94. Military History Now. June 15, 2013. Hessians for Hire- Meet the eighteenth century's Busiest 'Mercenaries'. Units. http://militaryhistorynow.com/2013/06/15/hired-guns-ten-amazing-facts-about-the-hessians/. Accessed 25 September 2014.

95. Minter, William. *Apartheid's Contras: An Inquiry into the Roots of War in Angola and Mozambique* (South Africa: Witwatersrand Press, 1994).

96. Monaghan, Andrew. 'Putin's Russia: shaping a 'grand strategy'?' *International Affairs*, 89:5 (2013), pp. 1221–1236.

97. Moore, Barrington. *Social Origins of Dictatorship and Democracy: Lord and Peasant in the Making of the Modern World* (USA: Beacon Press, 1993).

98. Moser, Harold D., David R. Hoth and George H. Hoemann. *The Papers of Andrew Jackson: Volume IV, 1816–1820* (University of Tennessee Press, 1994).

99. Motyl, Alexander J. 'Putin's zugzwang: The Russia-Ukraine Standoff,' *World Affairs* (July/August 2014), pp. 58–65.

100. Office of the Historian, Bureau of Public Affairs United States Department of State. Foreign Relations of the United States, 1894, Appendix II, Affairs in Hawaii. https://history.state.gov/historicaldocuments/frus1894app2/ch7subch1. Accessed 31 January 2019.

101. Olson, Mancur. *Power and Prosperity: Outgrowing Communist and Capitalist Dictatorships* (USA: Oxford University Press, 2000).

102. Organisation for Economic Co-operation and Development. *Supporting Statebuilding in Situations of Conflict and Fragility: Policy Guidance, DAC, Guidelines and Reference Series* (OECD Publishing, 2011).

103. Pesalj, Jovan, Nikola Samardžić and Charles W. Ingrao. *The Peace of Passarowitz, 1718* (West Lafayette, IN: Purdue University

Press, 2011); Showalter, Dennis. 2007. 'Hessians: The Best Armies Money could Buy'.

104. Peter, Labor Wilson. *Pirate Utopias: Moorish Corsairs & European Renegadoes* (USA: Autonomedia, 1995).

105. Raphael, Ray. *A People's History of the American Revolution* (USA: The New Press, 2001).

106. Reno, William. *Warlord Politics and African States* (USA: Lynne Reinner, 1998).

107. Reyna, Stephen P. *Wars without End: The Political Economy of a Pre-colonial African State* (USA: University Press of New England, 1990).

108. Robert, Layton. *Order and Anarchy. Civil Society, Social Disorder and War* (USA: Cambridge University Press, 2006).

109. Saivetz, Carol R. 'The ties that bind? Russia's evolving relations with its neighbors,' *Communist and Post-Communist Studies*, 45 (2012), pp. 401–412.

110. Salerno, Joseph. 'Imperialism and the Logic of War Making,' *The Independent Review*, 12:3 (Winter 2008), p. 450.

111. Sassen, Saskia. *Territory, Authority, Rights: From Medieval to Global Assemblages* (USA: Princeton University Press, 2006).

112. Saunders, Robert A. 'Is Vladimir Putin the super-villain we've all been waiting for?' http://www.e-ir.info/2015/09/22/vvp-is-vladimir-putin-the-super-villain-weve-all-been-waiting-for/. Accessed 3 February 2019.

113. Schelling, Thomas. *Arms and Influence* (USA: Yale University Press, 1966).

114. Schmitt, Carl. *The Theory of the Partisan: A Commentary/Remark on the Concept of the Political* (Berlin: Duncker & Humblot, 1963). English translation. Michigan State University Press, 2004. https://www.unqualified-reservations.org/archive/carlschmitttheoryof-thepartisan.pdf. Accessed 4 February 2019.

115. Shevchenko, Vitaly. "Little green men" or "Russian invaders"? *BBC*, 11 March 2014. https://www.bbc.com/news/world-europe-26532154. Accessed 22 January 2019.

116. Shishkin. Philip. Central Asia's Crisis of Governance, Asia Society. January 2012. https://asiasociety.org/files/pdf/120215_central_asia_crisis_governance.pdf. Accessed 3 February 2019.

117. Showalter, Dennis. 'Hessians: The Best Armies Money Could Buy,' *Military History*, 24:7 (2007), pp. 36–43.

118. Silverman, David J. *Thundersticks: Firearms and the Violent Transformation of Native America* (USA: Harvard University Press, 2016).

119. Singer, P.W. *Corporate Warriors: The Rise of the Privatized Military Industry* (USA: Cornell University Press, 2003).

120. Sivapragasam, Michael. *After the treaties: a social, economic and demographic history of Maroon society in Jamaica, 1739–1842.* Doctoral Thesis, University of Southampton, 2018.

121. Snelders, Stephen. *The Devil's Anarchy* (USA: Autonomedia, 2005).

122. Spruyt, Hendrik. 'Institutional Selection in International Relations: State Anarchy as Order,' *International Organization*, 48 (1994), pp. 527–557.

123. St John, Ronald Bruce. 'The Ideology of Mu'ammar Al-Qadhdhafi: Theory and Practice,' *International Journal of Middle East Studies*, 15 (1983), pp. 471–490.

124. Stichting Geuzenverzet 1940–1945. 2007. https://www.geuzenpenning.nl/index.php?tekst_id=4&lang=EN. Accessed 30 January 2019.

125. Stiff, Peter. *The Silent War: South African Recce Operations 1969–1994* (UK: Galago Publishing, 1999).

126. Stockholm International Peace Research Institute. 1. Armed Conflict. 2013. http://www.sipri.org/yearbook/2013/01. Accessed 2 February 2019.

127. Strange, Susan. *The Retreat of the State. The diffusion of power in the world economy* (USA: Cambridge University Press).

128. Streusand, Douglas E. *Islamic Gunpowder Empires: Ottomans, Safavids and Mughals* (USA: Westview Press, 2011).

129. Tareke, Gebru. 'The Ethiopia-Somalia War of 1977 Revisited,' *International Journal of African Historical Studies*, 33 (2000).

130. Taylor, Peter. *Indentured to Liberty* (USA: Cornell University Press, 1994).

131. *The Economist*, 'Putin's War on the West.' https://www.economist.com/leaders/2015/02/12/putins-war-on-the-west. Accessed 3 February 2019.

132. Thomson, Janice E. *Mercenaries, Pirates and Sovereigns: State-Building and Extraterritorial Violence in Early Modern Europe* (USA: Princeton University Press, 1995).

133. Tilly, Charles. *The Politics of Collective Violence* (USA: Cambridge University Press, 2003).

134. Trenin, Dmitri. *The Ukraine Crisis and the Resumption of Great Power Rivalry*, (Carnegie Moscow Center, 2014). http://carnegieendowment.org/files/ukraine_great_power_rivalry2014.pdf. Accessed 3 February 2019.

135. Turchin, Peter. *War and peace and war: The rise and fall of empires* (USA: Penguin, 2007).

136. Turner, John. *A Continent Ablaze: The Insurgency Wars in Africa, 1960 to the Present* (South Africa: Jonathan Ball, 1998), pp. 129–130. RENAMO continued to be known as the MNR or MNRA until 1979.

137. Unger, Roberto Mangabeira. *Plasticity to Power* (London: Verso, 2004).

138. US Department of State Archive. January 2009. Annexation of Hawaii 1898. https://2001-2009.state.gov/r/pa/ho/time/gp/17661.htm. Accessed 31 January 2019.

139. Using Targeted killing to fight the war on terror: Philosophical, moral and legal challenges. April 2011. University of Pennsylvania's 2011 conference on Targeted Killing. https://www.law.upenn.edu/institutes/cerl/conferences/targetedkilling/. Accessed 2 February 2019.

140. Van Creveld, Martin. *The Transformation of War* (USA: Free Press, 1991).

141. Vasquez, John. *The War Puzzle* (Cambridge University Press, 1993).

142. Vines, Alexander. *Renamo: Terrorism in Mozambique* (UK: Centre for Southern African Studies, 1991).

143. Von Clausewitz, Carl. *Vom Kriege* ("On War"), translated by James John Graham (London: N. Trübner, 1873). http://www.clausewitz.com/readings/OnWar1873/TOC.htm, Book 1, Chapter 1.

144. Walt, Stephen M. 'Alliance formation and the balance of world power,' *International Security*, 9:4 (1985), pp. 3–43.

145. Weber, Max. 'Politics als Beruf,' in *Max Weber: Essays in Sociology*, ed. and trans. H.H. Gerth and C. Wright Mills (USA: Oxford University Press, 1946), pp. 77–128.

146. Wikipedia. https://en.wikipedia.org/wiki/Fire-and-forget. Accessed 30 January 2019.

147. Wittek, Paul. *The Rise of the Ottoman Empire* (USA: Burt Franklin, 1971).

148. Working Together for Peace. 2010. http://www.c-r.org/our-work/accord/somalia/diplomacy-failed-state.php. Accessed 31 January 2019.

149. Zussman, Asaf and Noam Zussman, 'Assassinations: Evaluating the Effectiveness of an Israeli Counterterrorism Policy Using stock Market Data,' *Journal of Economic Perspectives*, 20:2 (Spring 2006), pp. 193–206.

INDEX

© The Author(s) 2020

D. Craig, *Sovereignty, War, and the Global State*,

https://doi.org/10.1007/978-3-030-19886-2